Unified Protocol for Transdiagnostic Treatment of Emotional Disorders

UNIFIED TRANSDIAGNOSTIC

✓**Treatments** *That Work*™

Unified Protocol for Transdiagnostic Treatment of Emotional Disorders

Therapist Guide

David H. Barlow • Todd J. Farchione
Christopher P. Fairholme • Kristen K. Ellard
Christina L. Boisseau • Laura B. Allen • Jill T. Ehrenreich-May

OXFORD
UNIVERSITY PRESS

2011

OXFORD
UNIVERSITY PRESS

Oxford University Press, Inc., publishes works that further
Oxford University's objective of excellence
in research, scholarship, and education.

Oxford   New York
Auckland   Cape Town   Dar es Salaam   Hong Kong   Karachi
Kuala Lumpur   Madrid   Melbourne   Mexico City   Nairobi
New Delhi   Shanghai   Taipei   Toronto

With offices in
Argentina   Austria   Brazil   Chile   Czech Republic   France   Greece
Guatemala   Hungary   Italy   Japan   Poland   Portugal   Singapore
South Korea   Switzerland   Thailand   Turkey   Ukraine   Vietnam

Copyright © 2011 by Oxford University Press, Inc.

Published by Oxford University Press, Inc.
198 Madison Avenue, New York, New York 10016
www.oup.com

Oxford is a registered trademark of Oxford University Press

Library of Congress Cataloging-in-Publication Data

Unified Protocol for transdiagnostic treatment of emotional disorders: therapist guide / David H. Barlow [et al.].
    p. ; cm.
  Includes bibliographical references.
  ISBN 978-0-19-977266-7 (pbk.) 1. Affective disorders—Treatment—Problems, exercises, etc.
   2. Cognitive therapy—Problems, exercises, etc. I. Barlow, David H. II. Title.
  [DNLM: 1. Mood Disorders—therapy. 2. Affective Symptoms—therapy. 3. Anxiety Disorders—therapy.
   4. Cognitive Therapy—methods. WM 171]
  RC537.U547 2010
  616.85'27—dc22

                                                        2010035312

9 8 7 6 5 4

Printed in the United States of America
on acid-free paper

About Treatments *ThatWork*™

Stunning developments in healthcare have taken place over the last several years, but many of our widely accepted interventions and strategies in mental health and behavioral medicine have been brought into question by research evidence as not only lacking benefit, but perhaps inducing harm (Barlow, 2010). Other strategies have been proven effective using the best current standards of evidence, resulting in broad-based recommendations to make these practices more available to the public (McHugh & Barlow, 2010). Several recent developments are behind this revolution. First, we have arrived at a much deeper understanding of pathology, both psychological and physical, which has led to the development of new, more precisely targeted interventions. Second, our research methodologies have improved substantially, such that we have reduced threats to internal and external validity, making the outcomes more directly applicable to clinical situations. Third, governments around the world, and healthcare systems and policymakers, have decided that the quality of care should improve, that it should be evidence based, and that it is in the public's interest to ensure that this happens (Barlow, 2004; Institute of Medicine, 2001; McHugh & Barlow, 2010).

Of course, the major stumbling block for clinicians everywhere is the accessibility of newly developed evidence-based psychological interventions. Workshops and books can go only so far in acquainting responsible and conscientious practitioners with the latest behavioral healthcare practices and their applicability to individual patients. This series, Treatments *ThatWork*™, is devoted to communicating these exciting new interventions to clinicians on the front lines of practice.

The manuals and workbooks in this series contain step-by-step, detailed procedures for assessing and treating specific problems and diagnoses. But this series also goes beyond the books and manuals by providing ancillary materials that will approximate the supervisory process in assisting practitioners in the implementation of these procedures in their practice.

In our emerging healthcare system, the growing consensus is that evidence-based practice offers the most responsible course of action for the mental health professional. All behavioral healthcare clinicians deeply desire to provide the best possible care for their patients. In this series, our aim is to close the dissemination and information gap and make that possible.

The latest development in evidence-based treatment programs based on the most up-to-date research and clinical evaluation is found in unified, transdiagnostic interventions for disorders that share common features and respond to common therapeutic procedures. Deepening understanding of the nature of psychological disorders reveals that commonalities in etiology and latent structures among many classes of disorders supersede differences, and many disorders in a class look very similar in terms of behavioral problems and brain function. Indeed, most people with one disorder or problem typically have another problem or comorbid disorder, often from the same class of disorders. Thinking of these disorders or problems as related, or on a "spectrum," is the approach now taken by leading therapists and researchers as well as the DSM-5 workgroups writing the next version of the diagnostic manual, which is due to appear in 2013. Treatment programs in this series are "unified" because they share a common, unified set of therapeutic procedures that are effective with a whole class of disorders, such as emotional disorders, eating disorders or addictive disorders. Treatment programs are "transdiagnostic" because they are designed to be effective with all of the disorders in that class (emotional or addictive or eating disorders) that someone might have, rather than just one disorder. Working with one set of therapeutic principles makes it easier and more efficient for a clinician to address all of the related problems with which a patient may present, in a more comprehensive and effective way.

This particular program is designed to address emotional disorders. Generally, this group of disorders includes all of the anxiety and mood (depressive) disorders such as panic disorder with or without agoraphobia, social anxiety disorder, generalized anxiety disorder, post-traumatic stress disorder, obsessive-compulsive disorder and depression. The program is also designed to address closely related "emotional disorders" such as hypochondriasis and other problems associated with excessive anxiety focused on health concerns, as well as many disorders where the experience of dissociation (feelings of unreality) is a principal complaint. What all of these disorders have in common, based on recent research findings, is excessive or inappropriate emotional responding accompanied by a sense that one's emotions are careening out of control.

The development of the Unified Protocol for Transdiagnostic Treatment of Emotional Disorders (UP) began with the distillation of key principles from traditional empirically supported cognitive behavioral treatments (CBT; e.g., Barlow & Craske, 2006) integrated with advances in research on emotion regulation and dysregulation (e.g., Fairholme, Boisseau, Ellard, Ehrenreich, & Barlow, 2010). It is important to note that the UP continues to emphasize the fundamental principles of traditional CBT as applied to emotional disorders such as extinction learning, through the prevention of cognitive and behavioral avoidance strategies, behavioral, emotional and interoceptive exposure, and the identification and modification of maladaptive cognitions.

This program is not generally recommended for a specific phobia, if that is the sole problem unaccompanied by other emotional disorders. Other books in this series can deal more efficiently with that problem (see Craske, Antony, & Barlow, 2006).

David H. Barlow, Editor-in-Chief,
Unified Transdiagnostic Treatments *That Work*™
Boston, MA

References

Barlow, D. H. (2004). Psychological treatments. *American Psychologist, 59,* 869–878.
Barlow, D. H. (2010). Negative effects from psychological treatments: A perspective. *American Psychologist,* 65(1), 13–20.

Barlow D. H. & Craske, M.G. (2006). *Mastery of your anxiety and panic (4th ed): Therapist guide.* New York: Oxford University Press.

Craske, M. G., Antony, M.M., & Barlow, D.H. (2006). *Mastering your fears and phobias (2nd ed): Therapist guide.* New York: Oxford University Press.

Fairholme, C. P., Boisseau, C. L., Ellard, K. K., Ehrenreich, J. T., & Barlow, D. H. (2010). Emotions, emotion regulation, and psychological treatment: A unified perspective. In A.M. Kring & D.M. Sloan (Eds.), *Emotion regulation and psychopathology: A transdiagnostic approach to etiology and treatment.* (pp. 283–309). New York: Guilford Press.

Institute of Medicine. (2001). Crossing the quality chasm: A new health system for the *21st century.* Washington, DC: National Academies Press.

McHugh, R. K., & Barlow, D. H. (2010). Dissemination and implementation of evidence-based psychological interventions: A review of current efforts. *American Psychologist, 65*(2), 73–84.

Acknowledgments

We acknowledge with deep gratitude the contributions of the following individuals to the development of the UP and the conduct of the initial clinical trial: Amantia Ametaj, Jenna R. Carl, Molly L. Choate, Benjamin Emmert-Aronson, Mara E. Fleischer, Meghan Fortune, Amanda G. Loerinc, Alex De Nadai, Johanna Thompson-Hollands, Zofia A. Wilamowska, and Carolyn Youren.

Contents

Part 1: Background for Therapists

Chapter 1   *Introductory Information for Therapists*

A Unified, Transdiagnostic Treatment for Emotional Disorders

Over the last several decades, many advances have been made in the psychological treatment of anxiety and mood disorders. Numerous individual treatment protocols have gained empirical support in targeting specific disorders. However, emerging conceptualizations of the major emotional disorders emphasize their commonalities rather than their differences; research points to considerable overlap in disorder phenomenology, a common set of diatheses, or vulnerabilities, to develop emotional disorders (see Chapter 2 for an expanded discussion), and generalization of treatment response to one disorder across other disorders. Thus, research lends support for a unified approach that considers these commonalities and is applicable to a range of emotional disorders.

Based on these advances we have developed a treatment applicable to all anxiety and unipolar mood disorders, and potentially other disorders with strong emotional components such as many somatoform and dissociative disorders. The Unified Protocol (UP) capitalizes on the contributions made by cognitive-behavioral theorists by distilling and incorporating the common principles found in existing empirically supported psychological treatments—namely, reevaluating maladaptive cognitive appraisals, changing action tendencies associated with the disordered emotions, preventing emotion avoidance, and utilizing emotion exposure procedures. It also draws on the innovations from the field of emotion science, incorporating and addressing deficits in emotion regulation common in emotional disorders.

For decades we have described anxiety and mood disorders as disorders of emotion (Barlow, 1988, 1991, 2002). Emotion regulation is a process by which individuals influence the occurrence, intensity, expression, and experience of emotions (e.g., Gross & Thompson, 2007), and this process appears to be an important mechanism in the development and maintenance of anxiety and mood disorders. Deficits in adaptive emotion regulation skills are a core feature of these disorders, as individuals with anxiety and mood disorders often use maladaptive regulation strategies that contribute to the persistence of symptoms. Thus, increased attention to emotional dysregulation in treatment is consistent with emerging conceptualizations emphasizing underlying commonalities, and is justified by current research findings.

Efficacy of the Unified Protocol

The latest iteration of the protocol was pilot-tested in an open trial of patients aged 18 to 65 with heterogeneous anxiety disorders, seeking treatment at the Center for Anxiety and Related Disorders (CARD) in Boston. Results of this trial are detailed in Ellard et al. (2010). In this trial, the UP yielded significant pre- to post-treatment effects across disorders, on a variety of measures. Using a conservative adaptation of algorithms to determine the clinical significance of outcomes in trials of CBT for anxiety (e.g., Roemer & Orsillo, 2007; for a full description see Ellard et al., 2010), 73% achieved responder status and 60% achieved high end-state functioning. Results improved further at 6-month follow-up, with 85% classified as treatment responders and 69% achieving high end-state functioning. Effect sizes obtained in the preliminary analyses appear at least comparable to those reported in similar trials of existing evidence-based CBT protocols (Barlow, 2008; Barlow, Allen, & Basden, 2007; Norton & Price, 2007), and a number of randomized controlled trials are underway at our center and around the world.

Who Will Benefit From the UP Program?

As noted, the UP was developed to assist people suffering from the full range of anxiety disorders and unipolar depression. While our most recent randomized controlled trial of the UP focused on the treatment of patients suffering from DSM-IV diagnoses of panic disorder with and without agoraphobia, obsessive-compulsive disorder, generalized anxiety disorder, and social phobia, the UP has also been used successfully in open trials to treat post-traumatic stress disorder, agoraphobia without history of panic disorder, specific phobia, hypochondriasis, and major depressive disorder. We would also expect the UP to be useful in treating symptoms of these disorders in patients who may not meet full definitional clinical criteria for an anxiety or depressive disorder, and who would then be categorized as anxiety (or mood) disorder not otherwise specified (NOS), as well as individuals subthreshold on severity criteria, but at risk for full disorder status.

What if Other Emotional Problems are Present?

Currently, the evidence strongly suggests considerable overlap among the various anxiety and mood disorders. At the diagnostic level this is most evident in the high rates of current and lifetime comorbidity (e.g., Brown, Campbell, Lehman, Grisham, & Mancill, 2001; Kessler et al., 1996; 1998). It is not at all uncommon for people with one anxiety or mood disorder to have, or to exhibit features of, other disorders. The presence of additional problems, however, does not preclude treatment with the UP. In fact, unlike single-disorder protocols, the UP was developed in large part to address the clinical reality of comorbidity, and can be used to treat co-occurring disorders simultaneously. This position is consistent with our initial research findings, which support the efficacy of the UP in simultaneously addressing additional problems in treatment (Ellard et al., 2010).

Assessment and Monitoring

Mental health professionals may wish to screen patients for the presence of emotional disorder(s) using the *Anxiety Disorders Interview Schedule for DSM-IV (ADIS-IV)*, which was designed for this purpose. This semistructured diagnostic clinical interview focuses on DSM-IV diagnoses of anxiety disorders and their accompanying mood states, somatoform disorders, and substance and alcohol use. The information derived from the interview allows clinicians to determine differential diagnoses and gain a clear understanding of the level and severity of each diagnosis. The *ADIS-IV* is available from Oxford University Press. Of course, a medical evaluation is also recommended to rule out medical conditions that may account for, or exacerbate, presenting symptomatology.

There are a number of additional standardized self-report inventories that can provide useful information for case formulation and treatment planning, and to evaluate therapeutic change. These might include measures such as the self-report version of the Yale-Brown Obsessive Compulsive Scale (Y-BOCS-SR; adapted from Goodman et al., 1989), the self-report version of the Panic Disorder Severity Scale (PDSS-SR; adapted from Shear, et al., 1997), the Penn State Worry Questionnaire (PSWQ; Meyer, Miller, Metzger, & Borkovec, 1990), and the Social Interaction Anxiety Scale (SIAS; Mattick & Clarke, 1998). Of course, there are many other good measures available that may be utilized in place of these.

For measures that cut across emotional disorders, we have used the Beck Depression Inventory-II (BDI-II; Beck, Steer, and Brown, 1996) and Beck Anxiety Inventory (BAI; Beck, Epstein, Brown, & Steer, 1988; Beck & Steer, 1990; Steer, Ranieri, Beck, & Clark, 1993) as general measures of depressive and anxious symptoms, respectively. Additionally, we recommend using the two non-diagnosis-specific measures of anxiety and depression provided in Chapter 3 of the workbook. These measures—the Overall Anxiety Severity and Impairment Scale (OASIS; Norman, Cissell, Means-Christensen, & Stein, 2006) and Overall Depression Severity and Impairment Scale (ODSIS), a measure we adapted from the OASIS to assess symptoms of depression—were developed as continuous measures of anxiety- and depression-related symptom severity and impairment that could be used across disorders and with multiple disorders.

Therapists may also find it valuable to examine functional impairment and quality of life. A number of reliable and well-validated measures exist specifically for this purpose, including the Work and Social Adjustment Scale (WSAS; modification of scale introduced by Hafner & Marks, 1976), Rand-modified Medical Outcomes Study 36-item Short-Form Health Survey (Rand MOS SF-36; Hays, Sherbourne, & Mazel, 1993), and Quality of Life Inventory (QOLI; Frisch, Cornell, & Villanueva, 1992).

Many patients presenting to treatment for emotional difficulties will already be taking psychotropic medications. In our experience, patients presenting to our clinic are typically prescribed low doses of high-potency benzodiazepines such as Xanax or Klonopin, or antidepressants including SSRIs such as Paxil or Prozac, SNRIs such as Effexor, and, to a lesser extent, tricyclic antidepressants. Issues surrounding the combination of medications with CBT treatments are not fully understood, and the most effective ways to combine medications and CBT has yet to be empirically tested. Thus, we do not recommend that patients discontinue medications before initiating treatment with the UP. Rather, we suggest that they continue on a stable dose of their current medications while going through the program.

Unless clinically necessary, we discourage patients from increasing dosages of medications, or from beginning new medications, during the course of treatment. When patients begin new medication regimens during treatment, it can be difficult to determine whether changes (either positive or negative) should be attributed to the medication (or side effects of the medication), the treatment, or a combination of the two. This can become confusing for the therapist and frustrating for the patient, and may ultimately lead to poorer treatment outcome. In addition, certain medications such as benzodiazepines, when taken regularly, may have a number of negative effects. They may lessen motivation to practice the skills learned in treatment and can dampen the intensity of emotions, making it difficult for patients to reap the full benefit of the exposures at the end of this program. If used to attempt to reduce emotional intensity (such as at the height of a panic attack), medications can also serve to support maladaptive emotional responding through negative reinforcement. For some patients, medications can become safety signals that may interfere with their ability to correct misappraisals of danger. Also, consistent with state dependency of learning, skills learned under the influence of the drug may not generalize to times when the drug is not present. Most of these problems are associated with high-potency benzodiazepines, and do not seem to occur with antidepressant medications. Finally, patients may attribute changes in treatment to any medication, thus making it difficult for them to gain a sense of efficacy in confronting feared situations. In turn, this may limit their ability to reduce or discontinue medications once treatment has been completed.

In our experience, many patients successfully completing the workbook taper or stop medication use on their own, without any encouragement to do so from the therapist. Nevertheless, Chapter 14 of this guide (corresponding to Chapter 13 of the patient workbook) contains information that may be helpful to patients who wish to discontinue their medications.

Who Should Administer the Program?

Treatment concepts and techniques are presented in sufficient detail in the corresponding patient workbook so that most mental health professionals should be able to supervise its implementation. However, we do have some recommendations for minimal requirements. We believe it is important that therapists are familiar with the basic principles of cognitive-behavioral interventions. Further, therapists should have a good understanding of the principles underlying the specific treatment procedures presented in the patient workbook. This will put therapists in the best position to adapt material to best suit the needs of each patient, and overcome difficulties in treatment should they arise. Finally, and most importantly, we recommend that therapists become familiar with the nature of emotional disorders; some basic information is presented in Chapter 2 of this guide, with recommendations for further reading.

Benefits of Using a Workbook

The first "revolution" in the development of effective psychological treatments has been the "manualization" of treatments during the past decade. These structured programs were written in sufficient detail to provide adequate instruction for therapists to administer them in the fashion that they were proven to be effective. The same holds for the UP, although this protocol focuses more on the administration of potent and empirically supported therapeutic procedures, as opposed to providing specific instruction on the treatment of symptoms related to a particular diagnosis or disorder. This does not imply that therapeutic skills are no longer required to achieve optimal outcomes. In fact, these skills are invaluable as the patient proceeds with the program.

The second stage of this "revolution" is creating a rendition of the structured program that is appropriate for direct distribution to patients who are working under therapeutic supervision. The UP workbook strives to be a good example of a scientifically sound guide, written at the patient's level, which can be a valuable supplement to programs delivered by professionals from a number of disciplines. There are several advantages to this as described in the sections that follow.

Self-Paced Progress

The availability of the UP workbook allows patients to move at their own individual pace. Some patients may wish to move more quickly through the program, by scheduling more frequent sessions, while others may choose to move more slowly due to conflicting demands such as work and travel schedules. Having the patient workbook available between irregularly scheduled sessions for review or rereading can be quite beneficial.

Ready Reference

While patients may seem to have a good understanding of material during the session, it is common for them to forget the important points, or to become confused, after leaving. One of the greatest benefits of the patient workbook is that it provides an opportunity for review of treatment concepts, explanations, and instructions between sessions. Further, it provides an immediate reference for patients when they are experiencing strong emotions. This can be important for the learning process, since going back to the information and using the skills "in the moment" can facilitate a greater understanding of the treatment concepts and a better appreciation for how these procedures can effectively be applied.

Availability to Family Members and Friends

Research at our center has shown that there is a significant benefit to having family members, especially spouses or other partners, be aware of and sometimes (under therapeutic direction) involved in treatment (e.g., Barlow, O'Brien, & Last, 1984; Cerny, Barlow, Craske, & Himadi, 1987). For example, in one study of patients with panic disorder with agoraphobia, patients whose partners were included in treatment did better at a 2-year follow-up than did those patients whose partners were not included. Similarly, research by Chambless and Steketee (1999) has shown that greater levels of hostility expressed toward the patient by relatives prior to the start of therapy predicted poorer treatment response. On the other hand, non-hostile criticism, or being critical of specific behaviors without devaluing, predicted better treatment response. A more recent study by Zinbarg, Lee, and Yoon (2007) produced identical results.

Family participation appears to be beneficial in several ways. First, when family members become more familiar with the nature of the disorder and the rationale underlying treatment, they can be helpful in overcoming avoidance behaviors. Second, having this understanding can also help family members stop behaviors of their own that may be detrimental to the treatment, such as unwittingly accommodating the patient's patterns of avoidance. Third, providing information to family members may help correct misconceptions regarding emotional disorders and, in doing so, reduce hostility and foster greater empathy, understanding, and compassion. Of course, some patients prefer that their spouse or family members be relatively uninformed about their problem and uninvolved in their treatment program. In these cases, the therapist may wish to speak with patients to identify any concerns they might have about sharing the problem with their partners, and to discuss the possible advantages (and disadvantages) of making this information more readily available. While we have generally found it beneficial to involve family members and friends, either initially or throughout the entire treatment, there may occasionally be times when it would be inappropriate to do so (e.g., severe marital discord). In these cases, we do not encourage the significant other's involvement.

Patients Can Refer to the Manual After the Program Ends

The UP workbook will help patients to deal effectively with emotional difficulties after treatment is over. As it is likely that many patients will experience a recurrence of their symptoms at some point following treatment, usually under times of increased stress, they may find it helpful to refer back to the workbook for helpful information on managing their symptoms, and hopefully prevent these symptoms from escalating into a full-blown relapse. Chapter 14 of the workbook specifically outlines ways for patients to maintain progress and prevent relapse. For many, the workbook may also assist them in making further gains once treatment has ended. As they move forward with new challenges, and continue to work on meeting their goals for treatment, they may very well find new meaning in the workbook material, and ultimately develop a greater understanding of the treatment concepts.

Full Workbook versus Installments

Some therapists might prefer distributing chapters from the UP workbook in installments, as opposed to supplying it in its entirety. This prevents patients from skipping ahead, and encourages a more organized approach to learning the treatment procedures. However, a potential downside in asking patients to piece the workbook together over time is that individual chapters are more likely to be misplaced. If this occurs, patients may end up with incomplete workbooks at the end of treatment, making it difficult for them to use the manual as a reference during the later parts of treatment, or after treatment has ended. Also, some patients find it useful to read ahead in order to gain a greater understanding of how earlier concepts may relate to later procedures and to provide them with a more general overview of the treatment program. In general, the more time patients spend looking at the workbook and thinking about the treatment concepts, the deeper their understanding of the treatment procedures and the greater their benefit. During the session, if patients mention material that they have read in future chapters, the therapist can simply redirect their attention to the current material and immediate assignments. Nevertheless, we do not discourage therapists from distributing the patient workbooks in installments if preferred.

Fees for the Workbooks

Typically, the cost of workbooks is incorporated into a program or therapist's fee structure in one of two ways. Workbooks can be purchased in bulk by the program or therapist, and these costs can then be incorporated into the costs of the therapy session or program. Alternatively, some therapists and programs, particularly those with a fixed fee schedule, may ask patients to assume the cost of purchasing the workbook themselves. In these cases, the therapist or program may wish to purchase workbooks in bulk and offer them for resale at the beginning of treatment.

Chapter 2   *The Nature of Emotional Disorders*

Empirical and data-driven conceptions of anxiety and major emotional disorders are emerging that emphasize their commonalities rather than their differences (Barlow, 2002; Brown, 2007; Brown & Barlow, 2009). Major developments in a number of areas support these conceptions. First, there is considerable overlap in how these disorders appear diagnostically, as evidenced by high rates of current and lifetime comorbidity (e.g., Brown, Campbell, Lehman, Grisham, & Mancill, 2001; Kessler et al., 1996, 1998, 2005; Kessler, Berglund, & Demler, 2003). Further, psychological treatments for a given anxiety disorder produce some improvement in additional anxiety or mood disorders that are not specifically addressed in treatment (Allen et al., 2010; Borkovec, Abel, & Newman, 1995; Brown, Antony, & Barlow, 1995; Tsao, Lewin, & Craske, 1998; Tsao, Mystkowski, & Zucker, 2002).

Second, emerging research on the latent structure of dimensional features of emotional disorders reveals a hierarchical structure that places emphasis on two core dimensions of temperament: neuroticism/negative affectivity, and extraversion/positive affectivity (e.g., Barlow, 2002; Brown, 2007; Brown & Barlow, 2009; Brown, Chorpita, & Barlow, 1998; Gershuny & Sher, 1998; Kasch, Rottenberg, Arnow, & Gotlib, 2002; Watson, Clark, & Carey, 1988). A substantial literature underscores the roles of these constructs in the onset, phenotypic overlap, and maintenance of anxiety and mood disorders (e.g., Brown, 2007; Brown & Barlow, 2009; Brown et al., 1998; Gershuny & Sher, 1998; Kasch, et al. 2002; Watson, et al., 1988). Also, recent research from affective neuroscience supports the importance of recognizing a broader based, more fundamental syndrome. Findings from this literature suggest that hyperexcitability of limbic structures, coupled with disrupted or limited inhibitory control by cortical structures, characterize individuals with anxiety and mood disorders and may distinguish them from healthy controls. These neurobiological processes underlie the increased intensity and frequency of negative emotional experience in anxiety and mood disorders (for reviews see Etkin & Wager, 2007; Shin & Liberzon, 2010).

Finally, a body of evidence supports commonalities in the etiology of anxiety and selected other emotional disorders, which has been summarized in the form of an etiological model referred to as *triple vulnerabilities* (Barlow, 1991, 2000, 2002; Suárez, Bennett, Goldstein, & Barlow, 2009). This model is described in greater detail in the next section.

Etiology

The triple vulnerabilities theory postulates an interacting set of vulnerabilities or diatheses relevant to the development of anxiety, anxiety disorders, and related emotional disorders (Barlow, 1991, 2000, 2002). According to this model, there is a common genetic contribution to the emotional disorders. Much of the research on this "generalized biological vulnerability" has focused on the genetic basis of temperaments labeled *anxiety, neuroticism, negative affect,* or *behavioral inhibition,* but this genetic vulnerability lies dormant unless it is activated or "turned on" by environmental events. Additionally, early life experiences under certain conditions contribute to a "generalized psychological vulnerability" to experience anxiety and related negative affective states (Chorpita & Barlow, 1998). It is this set of experiences, often but not always disruptive or even traumatic in nature, that produces a sense of uncontrollability and unpredictability that seems to be at the core of negative affect and derivative states of anxiety and depression.

If these two generalized vulnerabilities or diatheses line up, the individual is at increased risk for experiencing anxiety and depression in the context of stressful life events, which can activate the generalized vulnerabilities (Chorpita & Barlow, 1998; Suárez et al., 2009). But a third diathesis, referred to as a "specific psychological vulnerability," comes into play in the form of learning a particular focus for anxiety, or learning that some situations, objects, or internal somatic states are potentially dangerous even if objectively they are not. These early learning experiences can be as straightforward as watching parents model severe fears of specific objects or situations such as small animals (e.g., as in specific phobia), or more subtle, such as experiencing heightened attention from caregivers to the potential danger of experiencing unexplained somatic sensations (e.g., as in panic disorder with agoraphobia or hypochondriasis). We have proposed that these specific foci of anxiety represent the disorder-specific symptoms that may be relatively trivial variations in the manifestation of a broader underlying syndrome.

The Role of Emotion Regulation

An important concept for understanding emotional disorders is emotion regulation. By this, we are referring to the strategies individuals use to influence the occurrence, experience, intensity, and expression of a wide range of emotions (e.g., Gross, 2007; Kring & Sloan, 2010; Richards & Gross, 2000). Emotion regulation and dysregulation seem to play an important role in the maintenance of emotional disorders and become our target for treatment. Specifically, emotional disorders seem characterized to some degree by attempts to control both positive and negative emotions. Individuals concerned about the expression and experience of their emotions may attempt maladaptive emotion regulation strategies such as suppression or avoidance, hiding or ignoring them, with unintended consequences (Gross, 2007; Campbell-Sills & Barlow, 2007). Excessive attempts to control emotional experience lead, ironically, to an increase in the very feelings the individuals are attempting to regulate. It is this pattern that may erupt in a vicious cycle of increased physiological and emotional arousal, leading to more unsuccessful attempts at suppression or avoidance, which in turn contributes to growing psychological distress.

There is evidence that many emotional disorders are characterized to some extent by attempts to regulate (avoid) emotional experiences. Examples of this process in the context of depression, anger, and excitement (mania) are provided in Barlow (2002). The integration of concepts of emotion regulation and dysregulation into the theory and practice of the Unified Protocol are reviewed and updated in Campbell-Sills & Barlow (2007), Fairholme, Boisseau, Ellard, Ehrenreich, & Barlow (2009), and Wilamowska et al. (in press).

Chapter 3   *Basic Principles Underlying Treatment and Outline of the Treatment Procedures*

Basic Principles Underlying the Treatment Procedures

While the Unified Protocol (UP) is based on traditional cognitive-behavioral principles, its particular emphasis on the way individuals with emotional disorders experience and respond to their emotions is unique in bringing implicit cognitive and emotional processes to the forefront and making them available to fundamental psychological mechanisms of change. These mechanisms not only change behavior, including emotional experience, but also change brain function (and create new memories) (Craske & Mystkowski, 2006; Monfils, Cowansage, Klann, & LeDoux, 2009). The main premise of the treatment is that individuals with emotional disorders use maladaptive emotion regulation strategies—namely, attempts to avoid or dampen the intensity of uncomfortable emotions—which ultimately backfire and contribute to the maintenance of their symptoms. Thus, the UP is an emotion-focused treatment approach; that is, the treatment is designed to help patients learn how to confront and experience uncomfortable emotions, and to respond to their emotions in more adaptive ways. By modifying patients' emotion regulation habits, this treatment aims to reduce the intensity and incidence of maladaptive emotional experiences and improve functioning. It is important, however, to understand that the UP does not attempt to eliminate uncomfortable emotions altogether. Rather, the emphasis is on bringing emotions back to a functional level, so that even uncomfortable emotions can be adaptive and helpful.

In the early chapters of the UP workbook, patients are presented with a three-component model of emotions, which helps them develop a greater understanding of the interaction of thoughts, feelings, and behaviors in generating internal emotional experiences. In addition, patients are taught to track their emotional experiences in accordance with this model. This assists patients with gaining a greater awareness of the emotional experience (including the triggers and consequences of behavior) and helps them take a more objective view of their emotions, rather than simply getting "caught up" in their emotional response. The skill of emotion awareness is then further developed in workbook Chapter 7, which focuses on practicing nonjudgmental, present-focused awareness of emotional experiences. This awareness building is seen as an important core skill, serving to enhance acquisition of subsequent treatment concepts. As such, the UP emphasizes the adaptive, functional nature of emotions, and helps facilitate greater tolerance of emotions.

A second core skill in the UP consists of challenging negative and anxious appraisals related to external and internal threats, such as physical sensations and emotions, and increasing cognitive flexibility. We adapted existing cognitive interventions, as innovated by Aaron T. Beck (Beck, 1972; Beck, Rush, Shaw, & Emery, 1979), to focus on two fundamental misappraisals: first, the likelihood of a negative event happening (probability overestimation); and second, the consequences of that negative event if it did happen (catastrophizing; Barlow & Craske, 2000; Zinbarg, Craske, & Barlow, 2006). Also, unlike some other cognitive therapies, the emphasis of the UP is not on eliminating or suppressing negative thoughts and replacing them with more adaptive or realistic appraisals, but rather on increasing cognitive flexibility as an adaptive emotion regulation strategy. Patients are encouraged to use reappraisal strategies not only before, but also during and after emotionally laden situations. In addition, the UP emphasizes the dynamic interaction between cognitions, and both physical sensations and behaviors, as an important component of emerging emotional experiences. An introduction to appraisals and the procedure of reappraising negative emotional cognitions occurs in Chapter 8 of the workbook and usually is practiced throughout the remainder of treatment. Although cognitive reappraisal could theoretically be used as a standalone treatment procedure, our experience is that it is particularly important for assisting patients to engage in the interoceptive and situationally based emotion exposures that occur later in the treatment.

A third core skill in the UP is identifying and modifying maladaptive action tendencies, or emotion driven behaviors (EDBs), which is also a primary focus during exposure exercises. In fact, as first suggested in 1988 (Barlow, 1988) with regards to the treatment of phobic disorders, it is possible that one of the crucial functions of exposure is to prevent the action tendencies associated with the emotion and facilitate alternative behaviors. This is consistent with theories and evidence from emotion science that indicate that focusing on and modifying these actions can be an effective means of emotion control. As Izard pointed out in 1971, "the individual learns to act his way into a new way of feeling" (p. 410). The idea of reducing patterns of avoidance and changing maladaptive action tendencies is introduced early on in treatment, during the initial discussion on the nature of emotions, and is then discussed in greater detail in workbook Chapters 9 and 10.

Increasing awareness and tolerance of physical sensations through interoceptive exposures represents a fourth core skill in the UP. All patients, regardless of their diagnosis or specific foci of anxiety, are asked to engage in a series of interoceptive exercises designed to evoke physical sensations analogous to those typically associated with anxiety and distress. We first placed an emphasis on interoceptive exposures as applied to the treatment of panic disorder (Barlow, 1988; Barlow & Cerny, 1988), a disorder in which physical sensations serve as both a direct trigger and a specific focus of anxiety. However, in the UP, interoceptive exposures are applied across diagnoses, whether or not physical sensations represent a specific focus of the patient's anxiety, as a way to increase the patient's awareness of physical sensations as a core component of emotional experiences, as well as increasing tolerance of these sensations. Through interoceptive exposure exercises, patients begin to recognize the role of physical sensations in emotional experiences, identifying ways in which these somatic sensations might influence thoughts and behaviors, as well as how thoughts and behaviors can serve to intensify these sensations.

These core treatment concepts are brought together in the final phase of the UP through engagement in emotion exercises, a fifth core component of the UP. These exercises emphasize the elicitation of and exposure to emotional experiences in both situational and internal contexts. Consistent with other cognitive-behavioral therapies utilizing exposure, the exposure exercises occur in a graduated "stepwise" fashion, so that patients confront less difficult (and less emotionally provoking) situations before systematically moving on to situations that elicit more intense emotions. However, it is important to communicate that there is no necessary reason for conducting exposures in this way. More difficult situations produce higher intensity emotions, although intense emotions are no more dangerous than other emotions. With all exposures, the focus is on confronting the situation fully, so that patterns of avoidance and other safety behaviors are identified, and then efforts are made to reduce or eliminate these behaviors during the exposure exercises to best facilitate new learning and the creation of new memories. In this way, the tendency to engage in avoidance behaviors or emotional suppression is replaced with approach tendencies.

Description of Treatment Modules

Based upon the five core skills just discussed, the UP consists of five core treatment modules that target key aspects of emotional processing and regulation of emotional experiences: (1) present-focused emotion awareness, (2) cognitive flexibility, (3) emotion avoidance and emotion-driven behaviors, (4) awareness and tolerance of physical sensations, and (5) interoceptive and situation-based emotion exposure. Based upon traditional CBT approaches, these modules are anchored within the three-component, modal model of emotion (thoughts, feelings and behaviors) with an emphasis on increasing patient awareness of the interaction of each of these components, as well as the function of emotions and behaviors within the context of present-moment experience. Placing unfolding emotional experiences within the context of present-moment experiences allows the patient to identify patterns of responses and emotion regulation strategies that are inconsistent or incompatible with ongoing situational or motivational demands. Thus, the UP moves away from targeting disorder-specific symptoms and toward targeting the underlying mechanisms that exist along the full "neurotic spectrum" (Barlow, 2002; Krueger, Watson, & Barlow, 2005; Brown & Barlow, 2009). The five core modules are preceded by a module focused on enhancing motivation and readiness for change and treatment engagement, as well as an introductory module educating patients on the nature of emotions and providing a framework for understanding their emotional experiences. A final module consists of reviewing progress over treatment and developing relapse prevention strategies. As the treatment proceeds, the domains of thoughts, feelings, and behaviors are each explored in detail, focusing specifically on elucidating dysfunctional emotion regulation strategies that the patient has developed over time within each of these domains, and teaching patients more adaptive emotion regulation skills. For full details on manual development and specific modifications from earlier versions, we refer the reader to Ellard et al. (2010).

The modules build upon one another and were designed to proceed sequentially. However, flexibility was built into the UP by allowing each of the modules to be completed within a preset range of sessions, thus allowing for individual differences in patient presentations. For instance, individuals with excessive, uncontrollable worry might benefit from an extended focus on nonjudgmental present-focused awareness (Module 3), whereas individuals with repetitive compulsive behaviors might benefit from prolonged practice and attention to emotion avoidance and emotion-driven behaviors (Module 5).

Following is a description of the UP treatment modules and general guidelines for the number of sessions the therapist may wish to conduct for each module. As noted earlier, the number of sessions for each module will vary from patient to patient, depending on what seems clinically useful for a particular patient, and the therapist should feel free to modify as needed. We strongly recommend that each patient complete all of the treatment modules, if possible, even if the module may not initially appear to be directly relevant to the presenting problem. For instance, some patients do not report experiencing significant sensitivity to physical sensations and so, on the surface, interoceptive exposures may not appear indicated. However, it has been our experience that many of these patients still report some benefit from engaging in these procedures, giving them the opportunity to recognize physical sensations as an important component of emotional experiences. Again, flexibility in the session length of the modules provides the therapist with some freedom in how much the treatment procedures are emphasized for a particular patient.

Description of Treatment Modules

Module 1: Motivation Enhancement for Treatment Engagement

Duration: 1 session

Corresponding Therapist Guide chapter: 5

Corresponding Workbook chapter: 4

This module focuses on increasing the patient's readiness and motivation for behavior change, and fostering the patient's self-efficacy, or belief in his or her ability to successfully achieve change. Patients are given the opportunity to weigh the pros and cons of changing versus staying the same. Patients are also given the opportunity to articulate goals for treatment, with a focus on making these goals more concrete, and to identify possible steps for achieving their treatment goals. In addition, the companion chapter to this module found in Chapter 5 of this guide includes a series of therapeutic principles that are outlined for the therapist and that can be used throughout treatment to enhance treatment engagement and maintain patient motivation for behavior change. This module was incorporated into the UP based on research conducted by Westra and colleagues illustrating the efficacy of such techniques as an adjunct in the treatment of anxiety disorders (Westra & Dozois, 2006; Westra, Arkowitz, & Dozois, 2009) and is grounded in the principles and techniques used in Motivational Interviewing (Miller & Rollnick, 2002).

Module 2: Psychoeducation and Tracking of Emotional Experiences

Duration: 1–2 sessions

Corresponding Therapist Guide chapters: 6–7

Corresponding Workbook chapters: 5–6

The key concepts for this module include psychoeducation on the nature of emotions, the main components of an emotional experience, and the concept of learned responses. During this module patients are expected to develop greater awareness of their own patterns of emotional responding, including potential maintaining factors of such experiences (e.g., common triggers and/or environmental contingencies), by beginning to monitor and track these experiences.

Module 3: Emotion Awareness Training

Duration: 1–2 sessions

Corresponding Therapist Guide chapter: 8

Corresponding Workbook chapter: 7

The emotion awareness module is designed to help patients further identify how they are reacting and responding to their emotions, and practice a more nonjudgmental, present-focused awareness of their emotional experiences. In this module, patients are expected to begin developing skills to allow them to objectively observe their emotional experiences as they are occurring, within the context of the present moment, allowing them to work towards identifying specific thoughts, physical sensations, and behaviors that may be contributing to their distress. These skills are developed by practicing brief mindfulness and emotion induction exercises.

Module 4: Cognitive Appraisal and Reappraisal

Duration: 1–2 sessions

Corresponding Therapist Guide chapter: 9

Corresponding Workbook chapter: 8

In Module 4, the first of the three components presented in Module 2 are discussed. Patients are taught to consider the role of maladaptive, automatic appraisals in emerging emotional experiences. In this module, patients learn to identify their thinking patterns, practice ways to modify maladaptive thinking patterns, and increase flexibility in appraising different situations.

Module 5: Emotion Avoidance and Emotion-Driven Behaviors (EDBs)

Duration: 1–2 sessions

Corresponding Therapist Guide chapters: 10–11

Corresponding Workbook chapters: 9–10

This module focuses on the behavioral component of emotional experience. In this part of the treatment, the therapist assists patients in identifying patterns of emotion avoidance and maladaptive emotion driven behaviors (EDBs). After patients gain a greater understanding of how engaging in these behaviors maintains distress, they work to change current patterns of emotional responding.

Module 6: Awareness and Tolerance of Physical Sensations

Duration: 1 session

Corresponding Therapist Guide chapter: 12

Corresponding Workbook chapter: 11

This module focuses on increasing awareness of the role of physical sensations in emotional experiences. The therapist conducts a series interoceptive exposure exercises designed to evoke physical sensations analogous to those typically associated with anxiety and distress. The purpose of these exercises is to allow the patient to begin to identify how physical sensations influence thoughts and behaviors, as well as how thoughts and behaviors can influence physical sensations. Through interoceptive exposures, patients also begin to develop an increased tolerance of these sensations.

Module 7: Interoceptive and Situation-Based Emotion Exposures

Duration: 4–6 sessions

Corresponding Therapist Guide chapter: 13

Corresponding Workbook chapter: 12

This module focuses on exposure to both internal (including physical sensations) and external emotional triggers, which provides the patient with opportunities to increase their tolerance of emotions and allows for new contextual learning to occur. The focus of the exposures is on the emotional experience that arises in situations and can take the form of in-session, imaginal, and in vivo exposures. In this module, the therapist helps the patient design an Emotion Avoidance Hierarchy that contains a range of situations, so that exposures can proceed in a graded fashion for the remainder of treatment.

Module 8: Relapse Prevention

Duration: 1 session

Corresponding Therapist Guide chapter: 15

Corresponding Workbook chapter: 14

Treatment in the protocol concludes with a general review of treatment concepts and a discussion of the patient's progress. The therapist helps the patient to identify ways to maintain treatment gains and anticipate future difficulties, and encourages the patient to use treatment techniques to make further progress in achieving short-term and long-term goals.

Outline of the Treatment Procedures

The treatment is designed to be carried out in 12–18 sessions of approximately 50–60 minutes in duration. Sessions should be conducted weekly, although toward the end of treatment, the therapist may elect to hold sessions at 2-week intervals to allow patients more time to experience and practice overcoming residual problems.

The first four chapters of this guide provide introductory and background information about the treatment program. Subsequent chapters provide step-by-step instructions for facilitating treatment and conducting sessions. Each of these chapters corresponds to a chapter in the patient workbook as indicated, and is arranged as follows:

- A list of materials or forms

- Goals

- A summary of information from corresponding workbook chapter(s)

- A summary of key concepts

- A description of the principles underlying the particular treatment procedures

- Case vignettes that illustrate commonly asked questions or problems that might arise and examples of therapist responses

- Suggestions for managing atypical or problematic patient responses

- Description of homework assignments

We strongly recommend that you read the relevant chapter(s) in the patient workbook before that week's session, in addition to reading the pertinent information in this guide. Some therapists prefer that patients read the workbook chapter(s) before the session, so that the therapist can elaborate on issues and tasks, as well as answer questions. Other therapists prefer that patients read each chapter after the session is over, to review and consolidate the points covered in-session. We usually follow the latter strategy and assign the relevant patient workbook chapter(s) after each session.

Table 3.1 provides an example of how a therapist may wish to work through the chapters in the patient workbook. Again, the number of sessions for each of the primary UP modules, and thus the total number of treatment sessions, will vary from patient to patient, at the therapist's discretion. For example, a patient who worries constantly and has difficulty "staying in the moment" may spend more time developing awareness skills, whereas a patient suffering primarily from obsessive thoughts and compulsive behaviors may benefit from spending more time on the later treatment modules, as those modules are more directly focused on countering avoidance of feared situations and modifying maladaptive action tendencies.

Table 3.1 Sample Program Outline

Treatment Week(s) and Module	Workbook Chapter(s)	Therapist Guide Chapter(s)
Week 1 Introduction	Chapter 1: What are Emotional Disorders? Chapter 2: Is This Treatment Right for You? Chapter 3: Learning to Record Your Experiences	Chapter 4: Overview of General Treatment Format and Procedures
Week 2 Module 1	Chapter 4: Maintaining Motivation and Setting Goals for Treatment	Chapter 5: Motivation Enhancement for Treatment Engagement
Weeks 3 and 4 Module 2	Chapter 5: Understanding Your Emotions Chapter 6: Recognizing and Tracking Your Emotional Responses	Chapter 6: Understanding Emotions Chapter 7: Recognizing and Tracking Emotional Responses
Weeks 5 and 6 Module 3	Chapter 7: Learning to Observe Your Emotions and Your Reactions to Your Emotions	Chapter 8: Learning to Observe Experiences
Weeks 7 and 8 Module 4	Chapter 8: Understanding Thoughts: Thinking the Worst and Overestimating the Risk	Chapter 9: Cognitive Appraisal and Reappraisal
Week 9 and 10 Module 5	Chapter 9: Understanding Behaviors 1: Avoiding Your Emotions Chapter 10: Understanding Behaviors 2: Emotion-driven Behaviors	Chapter 10: Emotion Avoidance Chapter 11: Emotion-Driven Behaviors
Week 11 Module 6	Chapter 11: Understanding and Confronting Physical Sensations	Chapter 12: Awareness and Tolerance of Physical Sensations
Weeks 12 through 17 Module 7	Chapter 12: Putting it into Practice: Facing Your Emotions in the Situations in which They Occur	Chapter 13: Interoceptive and Situational Emotion Exposures
Week 18 Module 8	Chapter 13: Medications for Anxiety, Depression, and Related Emotional Disorders Chapter 14: Moving On From Here: Recognizing Your Accomplishments and Looking to Your Future	Chapter 14: Medications for Anxiety, Depression, and Related Emotional Disorders Chapter 15: Accomplishments, Maintenance, and Relapse Prevention

Chapter 4 | *Overview of General Treatment Format and Procedures*

Introducing the Patient to the Program

The goals of this treatment program are to help patients learn to better understand their emotional experiences, to ground them within the current context in which they are occurring, and to counter maladaptive strategies for managing uncomfortable emotional experiences, all in the service of learning to better tolerate "uncomfortable" emotions. When introducing the treatment program to patients, it is important to convey to them that the goal is *not* to eliminate the emotions of fear, anxiety, sadness, anger, etc. In fact, eliminating these emotions would not be very helpful because emotions provide us with a lot of important information when they occur in a functional, adaptive manner. Instead, this treatment focuses on bringing a greater awareness and understanding of the ways in which emotional experiences and responses to these experiences are contributing to symptoms. This treatment will also help patients become aware of the full range of experiences that elicit uncomfortable emotions, which may include both negative *and* positive events, and help them to learn more adaptive ways of responding to emotional triggers.

It is important to acknowledge that for many individuals struggling with mood and anxiety disorders, uncomfortable emotions are not limited to negative emotions, but may also include positive emotions. Positive emotions may actually be experienced as threatening, in that the patient feels "off guard" or vulnerable to an unforeseen catastrophe. For example, some people may find it difficult to allow themselves to let go of their worries and feel happy when something good is happening to them because they are waiting for the "other shoe to drop." Letting go of their worries and allowing themselves to be happy leaves some people feeling vulnerable. Others may find it difficult to enjoy pleasant feelings because they bring up thoughts of being undeserving or unworthy and, as such, experience these pleasant feelings as uncomfortable. Therefore, this treatment is designed to help patients become more aware of the full range of their emotional experiences, learn how to confront and experience a variety of uncomfortable emotions, both negative and positive, and learn to respond to their emotions in more adaptive ways. This treatment will help patients overcome maladaptive strategies they have developed in the service of avoiding intense or uncomfortable emotions—strategies that ultimately backfire, serving to prolong and exacerbate uncomfortable emotions and ultimately contribute to the maintenance of their symptoms. Ultimately, patients are expected to gain more control over their *responses* to their emotions, in order to prevent them from becoming excessive or overwhelming.

It is helpful to explain to patients that changing responses might be difficult, especially at first, as progress is not a linear process. Symptom fluctuation is natural over the course of the treatment, particularly when patients are asked to engage in more challenging tasks. However, the end result should be substantial improvement in overall functioning and responses to emotions. Inform patients that in the first few sessions, they will explore the purpose of emotions and the various components of an emotional experience. You will also introduce ways in which patients can begin monitoring their own emotional experiences as they unfold, as well as the ways they respond to these experiences. As the treatment progresses, patients will explore their emotional experiences and their reactions to them in greater detail, focusing on identifying responses that are ultimately not helpful and replacing them with more adaptive responses.

Your Role as Therapist

Ideally, your role should be one of a collaborator rather than an "authority." Both you and the patient must work together throughout treatment to design the most effective treatment plan possible. Changing patterns of behavior is difficult, and patients will need to give feedback regarding what is helpful and what is not, so that the most effective treatment plan possible can be devised and implemented. You should strive to gain a thorough understanding of the issues the patient brings to treatment and work to establish good rapport—both crucial parts of providing a strong foundation from which to introduce treatment concepts and successfully carry out some of the more challenging treatment exercises in future sessions.

Session Structure

Consistent with most cognitive-behavioral treatment protocols, sessions typically begin with a review of the homework assigned in the previous session. The homework review provides you an opportunity to briefly review with the patient the previous session's content, and link that content to what the patient experienced during the week since your last meeting. You should also use the homework review to assess the patient's progress and to inform the material covered in session. Following the homework review, you will present key concepts and conduct in-session exercises to assist the patient with understanding the treatment skills. This didactic instruction and interactive skill-building forms the main work for the session. At the end of each treatment session you will help the patient consolidate what he or she has learned. Ask patients to summarize the main take-home points or messages from the session, and ask if they had a negative reaction to anything about the session. Finally, you will negotiate the specific homework to be completed before the next session.

Homework and Out-of-Session Practice

Homework and practice assignments are assigned each week to reinforce the concepts from that week's session and to practice new skills. Research has found that completion of homework facilitates the practicing of skills learned in treatment, and is necessary in order to maximize the benefits of treatment. Thus, it is important to convey to patients that:

1. Attending sessions and listening to the concepts sets the stage for change.

2. Application and practice of the concepts in "real life" is what will lead to noticeable, lasting changes.

3. Every week, patients will be given papers to record assignments, and these should be brought to the following session to facilitate discussion about problems, setbacks, or obstacles.

4. Monitoring progress by charting the Overall Anxiety Severity and Interference Scale (OASIS) and Overall Depression Severity and Interference Scale (ODSIS) on the Progress Record will help the patient gauge his or her progress through treatment. Monitoring records can serve as both a powerful motivator and an important source of discussion during sessions, such as normalizing a patient's feeling that he or she has "backtracked" by reminding the patient that progress doesn't occur in a linear fashion.

At the end of each session, we recommend to patients that they read the workbook chapters relevant to the material that was discussed in session. Patients often find this process of review helpful in consolidating what they learned in session. Further, as you work through the treatment modules, you can have patients continue with homework from previous modules, if the additional practice is warranted. For instance, once the patient is introduced to the concept of present-focused awareness in Module 3, he or she can continue to practice these skills for the remainder of the treatment, if clinically indicated.

Homework Review

Beginning with the second session (or following the initial assignment of monitoring homework), it is a good idea to begin each session with a review of the patient's homework. Beginning each session this way serves three important functions:

1. Routinely starting the session with homework review reinforces the important role homework plays in the ultimate success of this program. If the patient is having difficulty complying with homework, address the issue right away, helping the patient identify obstacles to homework compliance and designing a plan they can stick to.

2. Reviewing homework allows you to correct any misconceptions or misunderstandings about the previous session's concepts, and provides an opportunity for the patient to ask any questions or voice any concerns.

3. Reviewing homework provides you with a rich source of information about the patient's ongoing experiences, which you can draw upon when illustrating subsequent concepts.

Patient Commitment

In order for this treatment to be effective, it is expected that patients will commit to and make time for the sessions each week. Urge patients to make the treatment sessions and homework a high priority. Remind patients that treatment lasts for a relatively short period of time, and making it a priority will allow them to reap the full benefits of the program and give them the opportunity to successfully achieve their treatment goals.

Dealing with Patient Ambivalence and Resistance

One of the most common difficulties that arise when working with patients is ambivalence about engaging in treatment procedures, including the completion of homework assignments. When patients do not readily comply with treatment procedures, therapists may assume that the patient lacks motivation for change. However, it is important to appreciate that in treatment we are asking patients to engage in the very tasks that they have had difficulty with in the past, and to confront physical sensations and other situations that are likely to produce intense, uncomfortable emotions. This can be challenging. As noted, resolving ambivalence and fostering a greater commitment to change is addressed in greater detail in Chapter 5 of this guide.

Review of Patient's Presenting Complaint

Prior to initiating treatment, it is necessary to gather a detailed functional assessment of the nature of the presenting complaint. While this is typically a continuous process involving a number of iterations, it begins by asking patients to provide a description of their presenting concerns. If available, it can be useful to use a diagnostic interview, such as the one described in Chapter 1 of this guide, to review specific areas of concern.

While conducting a functional assessment, be sure to identify the following key components:

1. The principal emotional experiences patients have on a daily basis (e.g., fear, anxiety, sadness, anger, guilt, shame, embarrassment, etc.) and how these emotional experiences affect their lives.

2. How these emotions might be interfering with patient functioning (e.g., how the patients are limiting themselves because of uncomfortable or uncontrollable emotions).

3. Any physical consequences associated with excessive emotions (e.g., fatigue, sleep problems, upset stomach, etc.).

4. Any techniques or strategies patients use to manage uncomfortable or intense emotions.

During the first few treatment sessions, it is important to gain a clear understanding of patients' presenting complaints and primary areas of difficulty, introduce patients to the treatment model, and begin building a strong therapeutic alliance. In addition, you will begin helping patients identify common triggers and contingencies that are maintaining their current patterns of emotional responding. It is not yet important to discuss these techniques critically; rather, you may just wish to reflect to patients that they use these strategies to reduce intense emotions in the moment. You may also wish to begin to develop discrepancy for patients by suggesting that these strategies have not been very effective thus far. For example, you could ask: "How effective has that strategy been?" or "How has this strategy been working for you?" As the treatment progresses and the patient begins to explore his or her emotional experiences and reactions to these experiences in greater detail, you can begin to reflect more specific instances in which the patient appears to be engaging in maladaptive responses to emotional experiences.

Part 2: Treatment Modules

Chapter 5 *Module 1: Motivation Enhancement for Treatment Engagement*

(Corresponds to Chapter 4 of the workbook)

Materials Needed

- Decisional Balance Worksheet
- Treatment Goal Setting Worksheet

Goals

- Introduce motivation and discuss its importance to outcome
- Help patient explore the costs and benefits of changing
- Help patient explore the costs and benefits of remaining the same
- Help patient set specific treatment goals
- Help patient set manageable steps to reach treatment goals

Summary of Information in Chapter 4 of UP Workbook

- Ambivalence is a natural part of the behavior change process. Motivation to engage in treatment will fluctuate throughout the course of treatment. Exploring pros and cons for changing, as well as for staying the same, can help resolve some of this ambivalence.

- Goals refer to future states or events that individuals are interested in making happen or hoping to prevent from happening. Some goals are achievable in a matter of hours ("going to the gym tonight"), while others might take longer to accomplish ("making more friends") and some are goals that individuals might always be working toward (e.g., "feeling happier").

- Setting specific, manageable goals has consistently been shown to improve the chances of successful behavior change. Identifying specific goals and then outlining steps to achieve those goals helps to keep motivation high and improves our chances of achieving our goals.

Key Concepts

In this section, the goals for the patient are to:

- Understand that ambivalence about behavior change is a natural part of the treatment process

- Identify pros and cons of changing

- Develop both specific and distant treatment goals

Motivation

Motivation and commitment are essential for patients beginning a course of treatment for emotional disorders. Homework compliance and engagement in treatment are consistently associated with treatment response and improved treatment outcomes. This module presents a set of therapist skills or therapeutic principles that have been empirically shown to help patients resolve ambivalence about change, and ultimately foster motivation to engage in treatment. This work draws heavily on the literature evaluating the efficacy of motivational interviewing among individuals with alcohol and substance use disorders (Miller & Rollnick, 2002), and from recent research that has adapted the principles of motivational interviewing for patients with anxiety and mood disorders (Westra & Dozois, 2003, 2006).

In this module, you will assist the patient in increasing readiness and motivation for behavior change through two motivational exercises: a decisional balance exercise, in which patients weigh the pros and cons of changing versus staying the same; and a treatment goal setting exercise, in which patients have the opportunity to articulate their goals for treatment, and are guided towards making these goals more concrete. Both of these exercises are discussed in more detail later in this chapter. Patients will likely benefit from the use of these techniques as an initial intervention, administered before beginning the core treatment modules presented in this guide. However, most patients would also benefit from the skillful employment of the basic principles of motivational enhancement throughout the course of treatment. For instance, before initiating emotion exposures patients might benefit from a brief review of their motivations for changing, or if patients experience a setback during treatment they would likely benefit from a therapeutic focus on rebuilding the beliefs in their ability to change. Therefore, before conducting motivational exercises with the patient, and in order to continue to use these principles throughout treatment, it is important for the therapist to have a clear understanding of the main principles of motivation enhancement. We discuss this in more detail in the next section.

Principles of Motivation Enhancement

As outlined in Miller & Rollnick (2002) there are four general principles underlying motivation enhancement therapies: (1) express empathy; (2) develop discrepancy; (3) roll with resistance; and (4) support self-efficacy. We will now discuss each principle in turn.

Principle 1 – Express Empathy

Stemming from the client-centered approach of Carl Rogers, the first therapeutic principle is to create an empathic therapeutic style to set the stage for change. This principle casts ambivalence as a natural part of the process of change, and encourages the therapist to respond to such ambivalence without judgment and, instead, with empathy for the patient's struggle. This response serves a number of purposes, including allowing the therapist to model nonjudgmental awareness of the patient's experience, and helping to align the therapist alongside the patient as they set out on the course of treatment together as collaborators.

Key therapeutic skills for implementing this principle include the use of open-ended questions and reflective listening. Reflecting the patient's struggle back to him or her demonstrates that the therapist is aware of *both* the patient's ambivalence and the desire for change.

Principle 2 – Develop Discrepancy

The very nature of emotional disorders suggests at least some ambivalence about changing responses to anxious and depressive symptoms, as the patient is at least partially aware of how the symptoms have negatively affected his or her life. However, changing these responses on the patient's own has likely been difficult, if not impossible. For example, a patient with obsessive-compulsive disorder (OCD) might recognize that the compulsive behavior is excessive, but at the same time believe that *not* engaging in the compulsion makes it more likely that a feared outcome or catastrophic consequence (the content of the obsession) will occur. Alternatively, a patient with generalized anxiety disorder (GAD) might feel very distressed about worry, but also believe that worry offers an important sense of control over anxiety. As mentioned previously, this ambivalence is a natural part of the process of behavior change. The therapist's job is to try to help patients to push the balance of the scales toward behavior change by amplifying the discrepancy between the patient's current situation and their ideal or desired situation. If an individual views current behavior as conflicting with important personal goals or values, the chances of modifying the behavior increase. Influencing the extent to which a given behavior is perceived as discrepant with one's goals or values increases the likelihood that the behavior will be changed. A number of specific techniques for helping patients to develop discrepancy and tilt the decisional balance towards behavior change are discussed in Chapter 4 of the workbook. Key therapeutic skills for implementing this principle include identification and selective reflection of statements or sentiments supporting behavior change.

Principle 3 – Roll with Resistance

A common trap that therapists sometimes fall into is arguing for behavior change. Unfortunately, this often has the unintended effect of the patient presenting arguments *against* behavior change. Treatment can then become a struggle between therapist and patient, instead of a collaborative process. In order to bypass this pitfall, the therapist responds to patient resistance or ambivalence not with confrontation but with acceptance of ambivalence, and attempts to elicit alternative perspectives *from the patient*. A guiding principle of motivation enhancement techniques is that change stems from, and is initiated by, the patient. From this perspective, resistance from patients is a signal for the therapist to help patients explore their ambivalence. This actively engages the patient in the problem-solving process and allows them to initiate their own behavior change. Key therapeutic skills for implementing this principle include validating patient concerns and using open-ended questions to invite new perspectives and facilitate problem solving by patients.

Principle 4 – Support Self-Efficacy

Research has consistently shown that above and beyond the intention to change a behavior, belief in one's ability to successfully change that behavior predicts actual behavior change. Thus, a patient's belief in his or her ability to successfully change the behavior in question, or *self-efficacy*, is a critical variable for motivation enhancement. Patients presenting for treatment often feel that they are unable to change their behavior on their own, or that they have already tried to change their behavior and have been unsuccessful. Therefore, it is essential that the therapist pay special attention to engendering self-efficacy for successful behavior change, in addition to increasing motivation for behavior change. This principle is employed throughout treatment by the therapist reinforcing positive behavior-change statements, and successful steps made or attempted toward behavior change. A number of more specific techniques or exercises for enhancing self-efficacy are discussed in the section that follows.

Motivation Enhancement Phases

As a general rule, motivation enhancement proceeds in two phases (see Miller & Rollnick, 2002). The four principles are used throughout both phases of this process. The first phase focuses on *building motivation* for behavior change, using the four basic principles of motivational enhancement previously described. This phase consists of techniques designed to identify important personal goals, highlight discrepancy between current behavior and personal goals, and explore the costs and benefits associated with behavior change. We use the Decisional Balance Worksheet to help patients build their motivation for change. The second phase focuses on enhancing patients' beliefs about their ability to successfully change their behavior (again, relying on the four principles of motivation enhancement). This phase capitalizes on the shifting decisional balance by enhancing patient self-efficacy for successful behavior change. Techniques used in this phase include setting specific, concrete behavior change goals, generating and exploring different plans for changing behavior, and committing to a finalized behavior change plan. We use the Treatment Goal Setting Worksheet to help patients strengthen their self-efficacy for changing their behavior.

Building Motivation – Decisional Balance Worksheet

This exercise helps therapist and patient directly address ambivalence for change by exploring the pros and cons of staying the same and changing. Once the patient has been given a sense of what treatment entails, he or she may become overwhelmed by the thought of actually completing treatment, which naturally triggers ambivalence. Even the most highly motivated patients can be expected to experience fluctuations in their levels of motivation over the course of treatment. For these reasons, it is helpful to have patients complete an exercise to help them become aware of and learn how to address some potential sources of their own ambivalence by completing the Decisional Balance Worksheet in Chapter 4 of the workbook.

Enhancing Self-Efficacy – Treatment Goal Setting Worksheet

This exercise helps patients increase beliefs in their ability to successfully achieve change by setting concrete, specific goals for behavior change. Research has consistently shown that one of the most effective ways to achieve successful behavior change is through goal setting. Goals refer to future states or events that an individual is interested in making happen, or hoping to prevent from happening. All patients will have goals related to the treatment, as well as other, larger goals for themselves in their lives. Goals can include more immediate things, such as "going to the gym tonight," "finishing my treatment homework," or "getting to work on time," and more distant things, such as "making more friends," "feeling more satisfied in life," or "finding a career I love."

Some of these goals might be achievable in a matter of hours ("going to the gym tonight"), while others might take longer to accomplish ("making more friends") and some might be things that patients will always be working toward (e.g., "feeling more satisfied in life"). Everyone has goals that are achievable in these different timeframes. Research has shown that setting specific, concrete, and manageable goals for behavior change greatly improves individuals' chances of successfully changing. Thus, the goal of "going to the gym tonight" is much more likely to lead to successful behavior change, than the goal of "feeling more satisfied in life." Before starting treatment, it is helpful for patients to identify the larger goals over the course of treatment, and then come up with more concrete, manageable steps to achieving those goals, by completing the Treatment Goal Setting Worksheet in Chapter 4 of the workbook.

Summary

Patient motivation is a necessary component of any successful psychological treatment. The four principles for motivation enhancement described in this chapter will help you maintain patient motivation throughout the course of treatment. It is important to convey to patients that motivation is not static and fixed; rather, it will fluctuate over the course of treatment. It is helpful to point out to patients that low motivation is not a sign that they have failed, but instead is an opportunity to employ the two motivation enhancement techniques of exploring the pros and cons of changing and staying the same, and setting treatment goals. These two exercises will help patients to keep their motivation high, or even increase it during times when they might be less motivated.

For more information on motivational interviewing, you may wish to consult one or more of the following suggested additional readings:

Arkowitz, H., Westra, H. A., Miller, W. R., & Rollnick, S. (2007). *Motivational interviewing in the treatment of psychological problems.* New York: Guilford Press.

Miller, W. R., & Rollnick, S. (2002). *Motivational interviewing: Preparing people for change* (2nd ed.). New York: Guilford Press.

Rosengren, D. B. (2009*). Building motivational interviewing skills: A practitioner workbook.* New York: Guilford Press.

Westra, H. A., Arkowitz, H., & Dozois, D. J. A. (2009). Adding a motivational interviewing pretreatment to cognitive behavioral therapy for generalized anxiety disorder: A preliminary randomized controlled trial. *Journal of Anxiety Disorders, 23,* 1011–1184.

Westra, H. A., & Dozois, D. J. A. (2006). Preparing clients for cognitive behavioral therapy: A randomized pilot study of motivational interviewing for anxiety. *Cognitive Therapy and Research, 30,* 481–498.

Case Vignettes

In the following case vignettes, T represents the therapist and P represents the patient.

Case Vignette #1

The following is a therapist/patient dialogue where the therapist is working with the patient to complete the Decisional Balance Worksheet by exploring the pros and cons of not making a behavior change (i.e., staying the same).

T: Ok, now let's look at some of the pros for staying the same. What did you come up with?

P: I left it blank. I don't really think there are any benefits to staying the same.

T: It's not uncommon to feel that way. However, what do you think has held you back from changing this before you came in to treatment?

P: Well, changing on my own was just so much work.

T: Changing one's behavior is really hard work. Especially when it's something we have practiced for so many years. It sounds like one of your pros for staying the same might be that it is simply easier to stay the same. Now, what are some of the cons for staying the same?

P: Well, the way things are kind of stinks. I mean, I can't do a lot of the things I want to be able to do, like travel or go out with friends.

T: So, some of the cons include being unable to travel and unable to go out with friends. What else were you able to come up with?

P: Mainly just that. All of the things that I can't do because of my panic.

T: You mentioned that one of the benefits for staying the same was that it was easier. How much work is it for you to try and manage your panic now?

P: It's a lot of work. In fact, it's pretty exhausting to constantly be on guard for situations that are going to make me panic.

T: It sounds like staying the same requires quite a lot of energy and effort on your part as well.

Case Vignette #2

The following is a therapist/patient dialogue where the therapist is working with the patient to set goals for treatment.

P: Well, I would really like to make more friends.

T: Ok, great. So, what would it look like when you've achieved this goal? What kinds of things would you be doing?

P: Hmm, I guess I'd be talking on the phone to friends when I'm driving home from work, going to see new movies with friends, having friends over for dinner parties, calling friends to cheer me up when I have a bad day, and not staying home alone on Saturday nights anymore.

T: Ok, those are some specific goals that you can work toward over the course of treatment. What are some manageable steps you can take to reach those goals?

P: I'm not sure. I guess I could ask for someone's phone number?

T: That sounds like a good idea. What can you do before that, to help make that step easier?

P: Well, I guess I could start by making small talk with people at work or the gym.

Managing Problems

When reviewing the Decisional Balance Worksheet with patients, it is important to ensure that they have honestly explored the pros and cons for both changing and staying the same. As illustrated in the first part of Case Vignette #1, one difficulty that comes up is that patients will sometimes leave blank the cons for changing or the pros for staying the same. However, it is important to recognize that there *are* benefits to staying the same, and identifying these potential obstacles early in treatment will allow the patient to be aware of them as treatment progresses. Once you have reviewed potential benefits for staying the same, it is important to launch a review of the cons for staying the same. You can also use any benefits the patient came up with to help him or her generate additional cons for staying the same, as illustrated in the second half of Case Vignette #1. Here the therapist was able to help the patient identify and respond to his own ambivalence, and also to generate additional reasons against staying the same. This technique can be helpful for overcoming patient ambivalence and continuing to build motivation.

When reviewing the Treatment Goal Setting Worksheet with patients it is important to make sure that the goals they have identified are reasonable and achievable. Patients will sometimes have problems identifying concrete steps toward the larger goals they have identified. It is important to make sure that the steps they have listed under the *Taking the Necessary Steps* section of the worksheet are in fact manageable. This is illustrated in Case Vignette #2. The therapist responded to a common difficulty by helping the patient to generate intermediate steps that he could work toward to achieve his ultimate goal of making more friends. In addition to modeling the problem-solving or goal-setting process for

the patient, the therapist also helped to enhance the patient's self-efficacy by reinforcing the patient's problem solving attempts.

Homework

 Instruct the patient to continue monitoring progress by
completing the OASIS and ODSIS forms and charting the
Progress Record.

Chapter 6   *Module 2: Understanding Emotions*

(Corresponds to Chapter 5 of the workbook)

Materials Needed

▪ Three-Component Model of Emotions form

Goals

▪ Provide an overview of the functional, adaptive nature of emotions

▪ Present the three components of emotional experiences (thoughts, physical sensations, and behaviors)

▪ Introduce the concept of emotion-driven behaviors (EDBs)

Summary of Information in Chapter 5 of UP Workbook

▪ All emotions at their core, be they positive or negative, serve an adaptive, functional purpose in our lives. They provide us with information about what is going on around us, enabling us to navigate our world and motivating us to do things that are helpful or useful for our survival.

▪ Our emotions signal us to engage in specific behaviors or action tendencies, which we call "emotion-driven behaviors" or EDBs. These are often automatic and adaptive.

▪ Emotional experiences can be better understood by breaking them down into their three component parts—thoughts, feelings/

physical sensations, and behaviors. These three components are present in all emotional experiences.

Key Concepts

The key concepts for this module include psychoeducation on the adaptive, functional nature of emotions, and an introduction to the main components of an emotional experience (thoughts, physical sensations, and behaviors). The goals for the patient are to:

- Develop a greater awareness of the important functional role the full range of emotions play in everyday life, including both positive *and* negative emotions

- Begin to view emotional experiences in their three component parts

- Start monitoring his or her own emotional experiences, identifying his or her responses to emotional triggers and situations in the three domains, and begin recording potential maintaining factors of such experiences

Psychoeducation – The Nature of Emotions

When discussing the functional, adaptive nature of emotions, it is important to discuss the following two main points:

1. Emotions are not necessarily "bad" or "dangerous," although they can sometimes feel that way. Oftentimes when people come in for treatment for emotional disorders, they want the therapist to "take away" or "stop" the negative emotions, or "shut off the switch" to the fear circuit in their brains. However, it is important for the patient to recognize that this would not be helpful or adaptive. Patients should understand at the outset of treatment that all emotions, positive and negative, are important and necessary at their core, even the ones we might view as uncomfortable or unpleasant. Patients will examine later in treatment how these necessary, adaptive emotions can become maladaptive or excessive,

but for now it is important for them to see how they function adaptively.

2. The primary function emotions serve (e.g., fear, anxiety, depression, anger, etc.) is to alert us to important external or internal events or situations, and to motivate us to act in response. We call the behaviors that occur in response to emotions *emotion-driven behaviors*, or EDBs, because they are driven by the emotion itself and are often hard to resist (or change) when we get emotional.

Definitions of Emotions and Examples of EDBs

To illustrate the adaptive, functional role of emotions, you may want to discuss with the patient in session the definitions and examples of emotions provided in Chapter 5 of the workbook. It is likely patients do not view these emotions (fear, sadness or depression, anxiety, and anger) as serving particularly positive or functional roles in their own lives, and may instead feel these emotions get in the way of their functioning. Using the examples to start the discussion, ask the patient whether he or she has ever had experiences where "negative" emotions have been helpful or useful.

Therapist Note:

■ *If the patient is having difficulty identifying instances when uncomfortable emotions have been adaptive in his or her own life, you may want to make the connection for the patient by reflecting examples of emotions and EDBs in the experiences the patient shared with you during the initial functional assessment.* ■

The Three-Component Model of Emotional Experiences

Patients often experience emotions like a big "cloud" of intense feelings, and find it difficult to determine what information (about the environment, situation, etc.) the emotions are trying to provide. Emotional experiences can actually be broken down into three main parts—what we think, what we do, and how we physically feel. By helping patients identify each of these parts, their emotions can begin to feel a bit less overwhelming.

The three components of emotions are as follows:

1. Physiological (How I Feel in My Body): These are the physical responses attached to emotional states. To illustrate this component, you may want to ask the patient the following questions: *"What physical sensations constitute feeling excited?"* *"What about when experiencing panic?"* *"Are there similar physical responses with different emotional states?"* *"What physical sensations are associated with depression or sadness?"* *"What about with fatigue, muscle tension, etc.?"*

2. Cognitive (What I Think): These are the thoughts often triggered by or linked with feeling states. To illustrate this component, you may want to explore these questions with patients: *"What types of thoughts do you notice when you feel depressed or anxious?"* *"What about when you feel happy?"*

3. Behavioral (What I Do): These are actions a person engages in or has the urge to engage in as a response to the feeling state. Often, someone will respond to a feeling without thinking about it. This is because it seems like our bodies just "know" the best way to deal with these situations. As noted previously, these actions in response to emotions are called *emotion-driven behaviors*, or EDBs. To illustrate this component, you may want to offer the patient some examples. For instance, someone who is depressed may stay in bed all day or just watch television, because the thought of getting out and "confronting" the day is too overwhelming. Or, someone who is anxious in social settings but suddenly finds himself in a crowd of people where he is expected to interact may quickly exit the situation to escape these frightening social encounters.

Case Vignette #1

In the following vignette, the therapist is helping the patient identify the primary components of their emotion and consider the adaptive function it might have served.

P: I guess I can see where anxiety can help you prepare for something, but when I'm anxious I just get so stressed out I don't feel like I can get anything done at all!

T: Can you give me an example?

P: Like last week, when I had to get ready for this job interview. I needed to find out more information about the company, and I probably should have practiced what I was going to say in the interview, but instead I just got so stressed out that I shut down and couldn't do anything.

T: So the anxiety about the interview motivated you to want to prepare by researching the company and practicing what you might say in the interview, but it also caused you to feel stressed. Did you feel tense?

P: Yes, my shoulders and neck get really tight and stiff.

T: And what happened when you "shut down?"

P: I just started worrying about whether I would come across as smart enough, or if I would seem like I knew what I was talking about, or if I would just blow the whole thing. And then I just got overwhelmed and couldn't think at all.

T: So you had some thoughts about what might happen—some doubts, some worries?

P: Yes.

T: And what did you end up doing?

P: Nothing. I felt paralyzed. In the end I was cramming for the interview the night before by just reading things off of their website. I didn't feel prepared at all.

T: So you reacted to your anxiety by procrastinating and not doing anything until the last minute. It sounds like you also reacted by worrying a lot and having a lot of doubting thoughts, and by getting physically tense. So whereas that initial anxiety prompted you to want to research and prepare for the interview, a whole bunch of other thoughts, feelings, and behaviors kicked in as well. We will talk more about these other responses during a later session, but for now let me ask you this: do you think that initial experience of anxiety that gave you the idea to prepare for the interview by researching the company and practicing was a good thing or a bad thing?

P: Well, I guess that part of it was a good thing, but then it just made me stressed out and overwhelmed.

T: So at its core, the anxiety served a good purpose, at least initially, even though it ended up triggering an uncomfortable experience for you. How that initial, functional purpose your anxiety served evolved into an experience you found uncomfortable and unhelpful is what we will be focusing on throughout this program.

Case Vignette #2

In the following vignette, the therapist is helping the patient consider the functional, adaptive nature of their emotions.

P: I guess I hear what you're saying, but I don't want to feel these things. I'm tired of being anxious and sad, that's what I came to you for!

T: That's right. No one wants to struggle or suffer through life, and that's what brought you here—to try and end your struggles. But as much as you don't like feeling sad or anxious, can you think of a time those emotions may have actually been helpful for you? Did you ever lose or break a favorite toy when you were a kid?

P: I don't know, I guess. I do remember one time I dropped my favorite action figure down a storm drain.

T: Can you remember how you felt about it?

P: Well, I obviously got really upset. I was only like 6 or 7. I remember I ran home crying.

T: So you felt pretty sad. What happened when you got home? Was anyone there to greet you?

P: My mom was there.

T: Do you remember how she responded?

P: Well, she probably gave me a big hug. I remember she tried to help me fish it out with my dad's fishing rod, but it didn't work.

T: So it sounds like your sadness motivated your mother to comfort you, and to help you cope in some way, by helping you try and get your action figure back?

P: I guess I never thought about it that way, but yes.

Managing Problems

Even though some patients may be able to see how emotions, even negative ones, can be adaptive, they may find it difficult to identify any time in their own lives when negative emotions were useful or helpful to them. If the patient is having difficulty identifying instances when uncomfortable emotions were adaptive, you may want to make the connection for him or her by reflecting examples of emotions and EDBs in the experiences the he or she shared with you during the initial functional assessment. As shown in Case Vignette #1, using a concrete example from the patient's own experience, and walking the patient through this example piece by piece, can help him or her to identify ways in which the initial emotional response may actually have been adaptive. It is not important at this stage in treatment to emphasize the distinction between adaptive and maladaptive aspects of the patient's experience, nor is it important to identify the patient's specific thoughts, feelings or behaviors that may have been maladaptive reactions. At this stage, the primary goal is to help the patient deconstruct his or her experience in order to identify at what point his or her emotional response may have been functional and adaptive.

✎ Instruct the patient to continue monitoring progress by completing the OASIS and ODSIS forms and charting the Progress Record.

✎ Have the patient complete the Three-Component Model of Emotions form in Chapter 5 of the workbook by selecting at least one emotional experience that occurs during the course of the week and breaking it down into thoughts, physical sensations/feelings, and behaviors. This form will help the patient build awareness of his or her emotional experiences, breaking down experiences in order to help them feel less overwhelming and unmanageable.

Chapter 7 · Module 2: Recognizing and Tracking Emotional Responses

---

(Corresponds to Chapter 6 of the workbook)

Materials Needed

- Monitoring Emotions and EDBs in Context form

- Three-Component Model of Emotions form

Goals

- Review homework from previous session

- Introduce ARC of emotional experiences

- Discuss learned responses

Summary of Information in Chapter 6 of UP Workbook

- A first step towards understanding emotional experiences is by monitoring the "ARC" of emotional experiences. The "ARC" of emotional experiences refers to the *antecedents* or triggers that precede emotions; *responses*, or thoughts, feelings and behaviors that occur in response to the triggered emotion(s); and *consequences*, both short- and long-term of these responses.

- Learned behaviors are behaviors repeatedly engaged in, in order to manage uncomfortable experiences. These behaviors often have beneficial short-term consequences, as they tend to reduce anxiety and distress; however, these behaviors often also have long-term negative consequences, such as causing interference in daily functioning.

Key Concepts

The key concepts for this session include a discussion of the antecedents (or triggers), responses, and consequences of emotional experiences, or the "ARC" of emotions. In addition, patients will see that we are designed to learn from our emotional experiences, and see how these experiences influence our behaviors. In this chapter, the goals for the patient are to:

■ Begin to identify triggers to emotional experiences, as well as his or her responses to these emotions and the short- and long-term consequences of these responses.

■ Understand the ways in which emotional experiences influence ongoing and future behaviors.

Homework Review

Begin with a review of the patient's OASIS, ODSIS, and Progress Record forms. Next, review the patient's Three-Component Model of Emotions form. Was the patient able to identify thoughts, feelings/physical sensations, and behaviors? If the patient has difficulty with any of these, help the patient to generate examples. Begin to demonstrate for the patient the ways in which each domain influences the others. Draw arrows connecting examples within the three components to visually demonstrate this point.

Introduction to Monitoring Emotional Experiences – The ARC of Emotions

The first step toward helping patients understand their own emotional experiences, and toward making their emotional experiences less intense or uncomfortable and more manageable, is by gaining a better understanding of when, where, and why they are occurring. This means starting to look more closely at their experiences, monitoring what is happening at the very moment in which they occur, as well as taking note of what happened before and what comes after.

Identifying the ARC of emotions is meant to introduce patients to the process of monitoring experiences with the goal of gaining a better understanding of what happens during an emotional experience. This will allow patients to work toward responding more adaptively and realistically. It is not important yet to monitor specific aspects of patient experiences, such as efforts to avoid emotions. Rather, the goal is to simply monitor emotional experiences and to become more aware of the context in which these experiences occur.

To illustrate the ARC of emotions, it is important to work through an example with patients, such as the ones provided in Chapter 6 of the workbook. When introducing the ARC of emotions, be sure to discuss the following four points:

1. Emotions don't just come out of nowhere, even though sometimes it might feel like they do. Every emotional experience is triggered by some event or situation, which causes a person to react and respond. In turn, these responses have consequences. Sometimes it is difficult to identify these triggers, but with repeated practice they can be identified.

2. The **"As"**, or *antecedents*, are the events or situations that trigger emotional experiences. Triggers can be either something that has just happened, something that happened much earlier in the day, or even something that occurred last week. To illustrate this point, you may want to refer to the examples of ARCs in Chapter 6 of the workbook. If the person in the examples (the one slated to give an oral presentation) got in an argument or was rejected by a loved one in the morning, it could influence the way he approaches the presentation at work later in the day. He may have more difficulty concentrating on the task at hand, or become more easily upset when the audience seems inattentive. The person may not have reacted in the same way if the argument earlier in the morning had not occurred. The "A" in this case would be both immediate and distal—for example, planning to make the presentation "perfect" *and* the fight with a loved one.

3. The "**Rs**", or *responses* to emotional experiences, include all of the responses that occur across the three main components of emotional experiences: thoughts, feelings/physical sensations, and behaviors. Patients often have difficulty initially identifying their responses in all three domains, so you may want to work through examples with the patient in session.

4. The "**Cs**", or *consequences,* can be short-term and long-term. The short-term consequences of emotional responses are often negatively reinforcing, causing the patient to engage in similar behaviors in the future. For example, when someone leaves a party early because they are experiencing a great deal of social anxiety, this response results in an immediate reduction in anxiety, which reinforces this behavior in the future. Similarly, indulging in an urge to check, for someone who has intrusive doubting thoughts, causes immediate relief from the anxiety caused by the doubt.

   However, in both these cases, long-term consequences are also evident. In the first scenario, a pattern of leaving parties early, or not attending at all, results in feelings of loneliness and isolation. In the second scenario, engaging in checking behaviors reinforces the belief that doubting thoughts must be neutralized by checking, which can develop into an intrusive, time-consuming behavior prolonging the time it takes to leave the house by several minutes.

   It is important that patients see both of these consequences of their responses—the short-term positive effect, and the long-term detrimental effect—as they are often in conflict with one another, and represent a poignant example of the disconnect between the lives patients would like to lead and the lives they are leading in service of managing their emotional distress.

Therapist Note:

▇ *Again, it is not important to discuss critically any emotion avoidance behaviors the patient might be engaging in at this stage of treatment. You will discuss emotion avoidance in more detail in Chapter 10. Rather, you may just wish to reflect to patients that the short-term consequence of these strategies is a reduction in intense emotions in the moment. You may also wish to begin to develop discrepancy for patients by suggesting that these strategies have not been very effective thus far in the long-term. For example, you could ask: "How effective has that strategy been?" or "How is that working for you?"* ▪

Understanding Emotions and Behavior: Learned Responses

The concepts in the preceding section should provide the patient with a better understanding of how emotional experiences unfold, the importance of increasing awareness of how emotions are triggered, how triggers influence responses, and what the short- and long-term consequences of these responses are. This next section expands upon the discussion of the consequences (or "Cs") of the ways in which the patient responds to emotional situations or events, by introducing the concept of learned responses.

When discussing learned behaviors, it is important to discuss these four main points:

1. We learn from our experiences. When we experience strong emotions, they leave lasting impressions. What triggers our emotions, and what happens when we have them, stays with us and influences how we experience similar situations in the future. We learn to repeat things that make us feel good, and to avoid things that make us feel bad. This is, at its core, adaptive, but can become maladaptive when the learned behavior is excessive or incongruent with the current, ongoing context.

2. We also learn to do certain things in order to keep ourselves from *potentially* feeling bad. For example, if spicy foods give a person heartburn, he or she may avoid spicy foods. Someone who doesn't want to wait in long lines at the supermarket may shop late at night or on a weekday afternoon instead. Similarly, if large social gatherings make a person anxious, he or she might avoid going to parties or other social events. If a person doesn't want to

experience a panic attack on the train, they may walk to work instead of riding the train.

3. Sometimes when situations bring up strong and intense emotions, we learn to do things to manage these emotions and then we keep doing those things until they become habit. For example, if engaging in conversations causes anxiety, the person may avert his or her gaze so as to avoid eye contact with the person to whom he or she is speaking. Averting one's gaze is a subtle EDB that serves as a means of escape, and can temporarily reduce anxiety. Repeatedly averting one's gaze during social interactions serves to strengthen this response, so that the person now habitually averts his or her gaze during conversations. Similarly, someone might check locks or appliances as an EDB in order to manage anxiety triggered by doubting thoughts. Repeatedly checking strengthens this EDB, such that now the person feels compelled to check whenever he or she leaves the house.

4. Whereas engaging in learned EDBs may seem adaptive, it is problematic because using EDBs to reduce the intensity of strong emotions can lead to a vicious cycle in which EDBs become stronger and better established, counterproductive, and insensitive to the true context in which the behavior is occurring. Avoiding these strong and intense feelings prevents any *new* learning from occurring, such as discovering the person's true ability to cope with the situation, or the reality that intense or distressing emotions will eventually lessen and fade.

Therapist Note:

■ *It is a good idea to make sure patients have a very clear understanding of the difficulties associated with avoiding uncomfortable emotions, and why trying to push away uncomfortable feelings may not be the best solution. It is important that patients begin thinking about these concepts, and begin to increase their awareness of how patterns of learned behaviors are functioning in their daily lives, particularly with regards to managing distressing emotions.* ■

Case Vignettes

Case Vignette #1

In the following vignette, patient and therapist are working together to identify the antecedents of the patient's emotional response.

P: How do I know what the "A" is? I don't always know why I feel anxious or irritable, sometimes I just do.

T: Can you give me an example?

P: Well, like the other morning, I just woke up not feeling "right" and I'm not sure why.

T: Can you remember what was happening that morning?

P: It was Saturday, so nothing was really going on. I'm not sure.

T: Can you remember what happened when you woke up? Did you get up right away, or did you lie in bed for a while?

P: I didn't get up right away; I stayed in bed for a while after I woke up.

T: Can you recall what you were doing when you stayed in bed, besides lying there?

P: Hmm, I'm not sure. I guess I was thinking a little about work. I had a meeting the day before, and I was sort of replaying it in my mind.

T: Do you remember any specific thoughts you had about the meeting?

P: I was wondering if something I said might have been misinterpreted by my coworker. I guess I was a little worried that something might happen when I got back to work on Monday.

T: So you were worrying about the outcome of your meeting the day before? Anything else?

P: I guess I was also wondering whether I should call my friend to make plans for the day, or if it was going to be too late to get hold of him.

T: How did those thoughts make you feel?

P: I guess I started to feel isolated, and started to beat up on myself.

T: What did you do next?

P: I didn't call my friend, and stayed in bed.

T: So, in this situation, if your "R" or response was negative thoughts about yourself, feelings of anxiousness and loneliness, and deciding to stay in bed, what do you think the "A" might have been?

P: I guess thinking about how I did in the meeting the day before.

T: Right! In this situation, you were ruminating about your performance, and worrying about the implications of your performance, which caused you to feel anxious and self-critical, leading to more negative thoughts about yourself, and driving you to stay home rather than call your friend. So, in this case, waking up ruminating and worrying served as a powerful trigger, or the "A."

Case Vignette #2

In the following vignette, the therapist is working to help the patient understand why her learned EDB is actually not helpful in the long term.

P: I don't see what's so bad about leaving a situation if it makes me feel better.

T: So you've left situations in the past, rather than staying and feeling bad?

P: Yes.

T: And how did that make you feel, when you left?

P: It got rid of my anxiety!

T: Right! And what about when you were in a similar situation after that?

P: Well, I've left situations a lot of times, if I don't feel comfortable in them.

T: And your anxiety has gone away each time?

P: Yep!

T: Sounds like a pretty effective strategy, at least in the short term. This is what we mean by learned behavior—it seems to work, so you learn to do it again the next time. What about long-term consequences? Are there situations you would like to be able to stay in?

P: Sometimes. Like my sister's graduation party—I really wanted to be there for her, but I didn't know her friends, and I was too uncomfortable, so I didn't stay.

T: Did you want to stay?

P: Yes! For my sister—I felt like I really let her down. I wanted to be there for her to celebrate.

T: So, whereas the short-term consequence of leaving the party was to get rid of your anxiety, it sounds like there were some other, long-term consequences as well?

P: Yes. I feel like I really disappointed her, and I feel like I missed out on her important day.

Managing Problems

For those patients who feel like their emotions just "happen" to them, or come out of nowhere, it can be difficult to identify emotional triggers. Help patients identify their emotional triggers by taking examples from their own lives and working through them to make them more concrete and specific. For example, if a patient reports that they felt "bad" on a certain day, help them to identify more concrete examples of their experience by asking what they were doing at a specific time, or to recount any exchanges they may have had that day with others. Use one of these more specific scenarios to map out the ARC of the patient's experience. When you are trying to identify the trigger, remember, the "As" can be something that happened much earlier in the day, or even earlier in the week, and can be something external or internal (e.g., feeling tired after a bad night's sleep). Have the patient describe the experience in detail, and work backwards with the patient to reconstruct the experience until you are able to identify the ARCs.

Similarly, some patients find it very difficult to identify the consequences of the experience. Ask patients to identify their responses to the emotional trigger, and how their responses made them feel immediately after. Most often, patients will respond that their actions had a positive effect, such as relieving their anxiety. It is important to acknowledge this initial, often positive result, as this is the key to better understanding learned responses and reinforcement. Additionally, because the result is often so positive, it is difficult for some patients to take a step further and identify ways in which these learned responses are negative, or at the very least serve to perpetuate their symptoms. Sometimes, by identifying what the patient values (such as being a supportive sister in Case Vignette #2), the patient is able to identify how her response to her emotions detracts from pursuing this value in the long term. These concepts are important for the patient to understand, as they serve to both explain why the lure is so strong to engage in emotion avoidance, and to illustrate why this approach is not necessarily working for them.

Homework

✎ Instruct the patient to continue monitoring progress by completing the OASIS and ODSIS forms and charting the Progress Record.

✎ Have the patient record at least one experience on the Three-Component Model of Emotions form in Chapter 5 of the workbook.

✎ Have the patient use the Monitoring Emotions and EDBs in Context form in Chapter 6 of the workbook to identify both short- and long-term consequences of his or her responses to emotionally distressing situations or events, as well as any patterns of learned behavior.

Chapter 8 | *Module 3: Emotion Awareness Training: Learning to Observe Experiences*

(Corresponds to Chapter 7 of the workbook)

Materials Needed

- Computer or stereo, music file or CD, and headphones for emotion induction exercise

- Nonjudgmental Present-Focused Emotion Awareness form

- Anchoring in the Present form

- Mood Induction Recording form

- Monitoring Emotions and EDBs in Context form

Goals

- Review homework from previous session

- Introduce nonjudgmental emotion awareness

- Introduce present-focused awareness

- Conduct in-session emotion awareness exercise

- Have patient practice techniques using a musical mood induction

Summary of Information in Chapter 7 of UP Workbook

- Emotion awareness skills as learning to observe thoughts, feelings/physical sensations, and behaviors that occur in response to emotions.

- Emotion acceptance as allowing emotions to occur without trying to change them or manage them in some way, observing and noting them for what they are.

- Present-focused awareness as an important skill allowing emotional reactions (thoughts, feelings/physical sensations, and behaviors) to be observed as they are occurring in the current context, rather than focusing on what may have happened when the emotion was triggered in the past, or what might happen in the future.

- Mindful, present-focused awareness exercises are introduced to allow the patient to begin practicing observing their experiences.

Key Concepts

The key concept of this chapter is present-focused, objective, nonjudgmental awareness of emotional experiences. In this chapter, patients will learn how to develop a greater awareness of how their emotional experiences unfold, with a particular emphasis on identifying affective reactions to emotions or judgments about emotions. Patients will learn how to identify primary and secondary emotions, and will practice taking a nonjudgmental, present-focused approach to their emotional experiences using brief mindfulness and emotion induction exercises. In this chapter, the goals for the patient are to:

- Learn how to observe his or her emotional experiences in an objective, nonjudgmental way.

- Develop skills to help him or her observe emotional experiences within the context of the present moment.

- Begin developing a conditioned cue to help shift his or her attention to the present moment.

Homework Review

Begin with a review of the patient's OASIS, ODSIS, and Progress Record forms, as well the Three-Component Model of Emotions form. Was the patient able to identify triggers to his or her emotions? Did the patient record thoughts, feelings and behaviors? It may be helpful to work through examples with patients and help them identify responses in all three of these domains if they are having difficulty on their own. Also, review the patient's Monitoring Emotions and EDBs in Context form. Was the patient able to identify both short- and long-term consequences of his or her responses? You may want to use this form to begin a discussion of the concepts in this chapter, and refer back to the patient's examples to illustrate and reinforce main concepts.

Introduction to Nonjudgmental, Present-Focused Emotion Awareness

Importance of Emotion Awareness

In this session you will introduce the concept of emotion awareness to the patient. The patient might feel like he or she is already keenly aware of his or her emotions, but the emotions might seem confusing, or seem to just "happen" automatically as a result of some situation or event or memory. However, in this session you will discuss a different quality of awareness, providing the patient with skills to become a more objective observer of his or her experiences. This is an important skill for the patient to acquire early on in treatment, and will facilitate acquisition of later treatment concepts. The ability to objectively observe emotional experiences as they are occurring in the moment will allow the patient to better identify and alter maladaptive thoughts and behaviors, as well as recognize when and how feelings/physical sensations are triggered by, or serve as triggers for, maladaptive thoughts and behaviors. When introducing emotion awareness, it is important to briefly discuss these three main points, which you will later discuss in greater detail:

1. *Primary emotions* are the "first" emotional reactions to a situation or memory. These emotions are often functional and directly related to the cues in the situation or memory. However, *secondary reactions* are the ways we respond to the primary emotions, and these reactions are what typically lead to disordered emotions.

2. Secondary reactions to emotions tend to be judgment-laden, such as when someone interprets anxiety as a sign that he or she can't

cope with the current situation, or interpreting sadness as a sign that he or she is a failure or the situation is hopeless.

3. Secondary reactions to emotions are often not based upon information from the present-moment context. They are often based upon what has happened before, or thoughts about what might happen in the future. This can prevent the person from perceiving potential corrective information from the current, ongoing context.

Reactions to Emotions

Note that within every emotional experience there is an initial emotion triggered by some event or memory, which is then followed by a reaction to this emotion. Often this initial, primary emotion, such as a sudden surge of fear in response to an unexpected noise, is not problematic in and of itself. However, the way a person responds to this initial emotion, called *secondary reactions,* can become problematic, such as thinking catastrophic thoughts about what might have made the sound, which serves to increase anxiety, causes the heart to beat faster, muscles to tense, and drives a person to seek reassurance. These reactions can color, influence, and motivate interpretations of, and actions in response to, emotional experiences. Explain to the patient that emotion awareness involves not only paying attention to emotional experiences, but also being aware of *reactions to* these emotional experiences.

Judgments about Emotions

Secondary reactions quite often carry with them an evaluative, critical, or judgmental tone, such as "this feeling is bad" or "the way I am feeling means I am incompetent in this situation." Additionally, it is important to recognize that the rejection of emotional experiences is not always limited to negative emotions. Sometimes, people react negatively to *positive* emotional experiences as well, finding them threatening or anxiety provoking, viewing them as an indication that they have been taken off guard, or are more vulnerable to something bad happening.

When judgments are placed on emotional experiences, the person often loses touch with what purpose the primary emotion is intended to serve (e.g., experiencing the primary emotion of fear after hearing an unexpected sound, which then alerts us to something in the environment that may or may not be threatening). Secondary reactions can lead us to view primary emotions as something threatening and unwanted, instead of being nature's clever way of signaling to us what is going on in our world *right now*. Many people with anxiety and depressive disorders view any sort of negative or positive emotion (fear, sadness, anxiety, joy) as inherently threatening and aversive, often interpreting them as having catastrophic implications, rather than as transient experiences. Cultivating objective, nonjudgmental awareness allows the patient to better identify catastrophic or maladaptive interpretations of his or her emotions, as well as maladaptive behavioral responses to them.

Therapist Note:

■ *You may want to guide the patient through an example of a situation that brought up a strong emotional response, preferably using an example from the patient's homework forms. Help the patient identify the primary emotion, as well as the secondary reactions to this emotion. Use the Three-Component Model of Emotions form to help the patient map out the emotional experience, using arrows to show how reactions in one domain influenced reactions in another (e.g., a catastrophic thought leading to an increase in anxiety and muscle tension). Ask the patient to describe his or her reactions to the emotions, gently pointing out when evaluative, judgmental phrases are used.*

To illustrate a nonjudgmental approach to emotional experiences, it may be helpful to engage the patient in an exercise. Have the patient imagine how he or she would respond to a friend who revealed they were feeling a particularly uncomfortable emotion. Would the patient say the friend was "stupid" or "wrong" for feeling that way?

Or would the patient have some empathy for the friend's experience? Suggest the patient practice this same perspective with his or her own feelings.

Importance of Present Focus

In addition to emphasizing taking an objective, nonjudgmental stance on emotional experiences, introduce the patient to the concept of present-focused, mindful awareness, and give two exercises to practice this skill. The rationale for an emphasis on present-focused awareness lies in the fact that many of the reactions patients have to their emotions are based upon memories and associations with past situations or events, and/or anticipation of potential future consequences or outcomes. Often patients are not paying attention to the current context in which their emotions are occurring, and thus are missing out on valuable corrective information. For example, a patient with panic disorder who is experiencing dizziness or lightheadedness may be focusing on the fact that the last time she had these physical sensations she experienced a full-blown panic attack, or she might be focusing on the impending panic attack she believes will "inevitably" follow the physical sensations. What the patient is not focusing on is the potentially corrective information that, even though she is experiencing similar physical sensations, at that moment she is not having a panic attack. Similarly, a patient with generalized anxiety disorder may be so focused on a potentially catastrophic future outcome, such as being broke and alone, that he or she misses the fact that at that moment they are neither broke nor alone, and have actually been surviving quite well. This process of refocusing awareness and attention to the present moment is called being mindful of our experiences.

When discussing present-focused awareness with patients, it is important to emphasize these three main points:

1. Practicing present-focused, mindful awareness may feel awkward at first. Some patients find it particularly difficult to observe their thoughts without engaging with them or getting "carried away" by them. Remind patients that the goal is not to do these exercises

perfectly – the goal is to become better at observing their experience as it is happening in the present moment. Encourage patients to try formally practicing mindful awareness once per day for at least one week, in order to get more comfortable with it. You can describe this skill as developing a new muscle – only through repeated practice will the muscle gain strength and the process become automatic.

2. In addition to formal practice using the Nonjudgmental Present-Focused Emotional Awareness form in Chapter 7 of the workbook (discussed in more detail later), encourage patients to engage in brief mindful exercises throughout the day, as described on the Anchoring in the Present form (also in Chapter 7 of the workbook). Patients should use these exercises to help develop a habit that can be used to quickly shift their attention to the present moment during times of distress. To facilitate this process, help the patient identify some "cue" he or she can use in conjunction with these brief exercises that will eventually become associated with a way to anchor in the present moment. One very useful (and portable!) cue is breath. Pairing a deep breath with a shift in attention onto something tangible occurring in the present moment (such as listening to cars passing by or the sound of a bird) can condition the breath to serve as a powerful cue to remind the patient to focus on the present moment. Be sure to point out to the patient that the breath should not be used as a distraction or relaxation technique. Rather, the breath should serve as a reminder to the patient to focus on what is going on *at that moment.*

3. Once the patient has identified a cue, encourage him or her to use this cue during times of distress to help shift attention to the present moment. In addition, immediately following this cue, and once attention is brought back to the present context, patients should do a quick "three-point check" to objectively and nonjudgmentally observe their current, ongoing reactions within each of the three domains of emotional experiences. Tell the patient to ask him or herself, "What are my thoughts *right now?* What emotions and physical sensations am I experiencing *right now?* What am I doing *right now?*" The patient should use this three-point check to identify any maladaptive thoughts, behaviors, or reactions and replace them

with more adaptive responses. Explain to the patient that these concepts—identifying maladaptive responses in each domain and replacing them with adaptive responses – will be covered in detail over the next several sessions, but for now the goal is to practice being an objective observer of experience.

Demonstration of Present-Focused, Nonjudgmental Awareness

In order for patients to fully understand the concepts presented in this session, it is essential for them to practice them, or learn by doing. Patients should first engage in this practice by paying attention to their emotional experiences in a present-focused, nonjudgmental manner by running through a brief mindfulness exercise. This skill should then be practiced while in an emotional state, using an emotion induction exercise, in order to allow the patients to utilize these skills in an emotionally provoking situation.

Practicing Nonjudgmental Emotion Awareness

Have the patient practice present-focused, nonjudgmental awareness by conducting a brief mindfulness exercise. Choose an exercise you feel is most appropriate for the patient. You may choose to use the exercise in the workbook, or you may choose another of the suggested exercises found on the companion website for this guide at www.oup.com/us/ttw. Inform the patient that during this exercise he or she should practice paying attention to what is happening inside and around him or her *at this very moment* in an objective way, acknowledging any thoughts, feelings, and behaviors, just as they are, letting go of the need to critically judge, change, or avoid the experience. If the patient is finding it difficult to stay focused in the moment, or finds his or her mind wandering, encourage the patient to practice using the chosen cue (such as the breath) to help bring attention back to the present and back to objective observation of experience.

If you choose to use the exercise in the workbook, try to keep a steady, comfortable pace, talking slowly and pausing frequently to allow the patient the opportunity to observe the experience. Be sure to process the exercise with the patient afterwards. You may want to use the Three-Component Model of Emotions form to help the patient map out reactions and responses to the exercise. Reflect any maladaptive or judgmental responses to the patient, without correcting them at this time. Remind the patient that over the coming weeks you will work together to explore each of the three domains (thoughts, feelings, and behaviors) in greater detail, but for now the goal is to observe and notice the experience.

Emotion Induction Exercise

Once the patient has had the opportunity to practice present-focused, objective awareness using a formal mindfulness exercise, it is beneficial to practice this same skill in the context of an emotional experience. The purpose of learning this skill is to be able to use it during times of distress to gain an objective, nonjudgmental perspective, and use potential corrective information from the current context to help alter maladaptive responses.

The following is an example of an exercise that can be used:

Have the patient identify a piece of music that brings up emotions, memories, or strong reactions. If the patient is unable to identify a piece of music, you may want to choose something from the list of suggestions provided online at www.oup.com/us/ttw. In our center, we have done this exercise in two ways. Either:

1. The patient brings in a CD or music player (e.g., iPod) which is connected to stereo speakers or headphones during the session.

   Or

2. Using iTunes or another downloadable music site, the selected song is downloaded onto the therapist's own computer and played during session.

Using the selected piece of music, have the patient practice observing his or her experience by noticing thoughts, feelings, and reactions, much in the same way as during the mindfulness exercise. Remind patients that the goal of this exercise is to practice being fully aware of their emotional experiences *as they are occurring right now in the present moment*, without labeling or judging. Also remind patients if they find themselves getting stuck they can use their breath (or other chosen cue) to help anchor themselves to the present. At the conclusion of the music, assist patients in eliciting thoughts, feelings, or other reactions, helping them observe these reactions in objective, nonjudgmental ways.

Case Vignettes

Case Vignette #1

In the following vignette, the therapist is introducing the patient to the concept of mindfulness.

P: This feels a little "new age-y." I'm not really into that sort of thing.

T: It is true, the idea of mindfulness meditation has its roots in practices like Buddhism, and the idea of practicing something related to Eastern mysticism can feel uncomfortable to some people. What we are asking you to do here is not to become a Buddhist, or even a formal "meditator" or someone you are not comfortable being. (Although some people do find the practice of meditation so helpful that they begin to practice it in their daily life.) Instead, we have found that the principle objective of mindfulness meditation—shifting your attention from being caught up "in your head" to an objective, observing perspective on your experience—is incredibly helpful for both understanding your experience, and for recognizing when and how you might be reacting to your experience in ways that are making things worse. For example, when you feel anxious, and then begin to have a lot of really harsh, critical thoughts about yourself for being anxious, those thoughts are making you feel worse. Taking a nonjudgmental, objective stance will help you to begin to separate out your anxiety from your harsh critical reaction to it, giving you the opportunity to stop the cycle before it starts. Doing these formal mindfulness exercises now allows you to practice what it feels like to observe your experience in this way, giving you a powerful tool for coping with uncomfortable emotional experiences.

In the following case vignette, the therapist is helping the patient understand the benefits of observing experiences in the present moment.

P: I don't like to sit still, it makes me more anxious.

T: Tell me more–what happens when you sit still.

P: I don't know. I just feel like I should be doing something. I feel like if I let myself stop thinking about everything I need to do my whole day will fall apart. I'm also afraid I'll start thinking about things I'd really rather not think about.

T: So, by sitting still and focusing on the present, you are afraid you will be losing control of things that are supposed to happen during your day, and you might start thinking about things that have happened in the past?

P: Yeah, and that just makes me even more anxious.

T: Tell me what you are thinking about the things you need to do later today.

P: Well, I'm worried that I'll be late for my doctor's appointment, and that I won't get the car back to my husband in time this afternoon, and that he will be late for his meeting which would be really bad.

T: And where are you right now?

P: I'm here in this office.

T: Are you running late right now?

P: No, unless we run over.

T: Are we running over?

P: Well, not right now.

T: So, you are not late for anything at the moment, but you are focusing on the possibility that you might be late later on. How does focusing on the possibility you might be late later on make you feel?

P: Anxious!

T: And what about the information that right now, in this moment, you are not running late?

P: Well, much less anxious. But I still could run late later!

T: Does thinking about being late later, or noticing that you are not late now, change what is going to happen in three hours time?

P: I don't know, it depends on what happens later!

T: Right! So, you really have no way of knowing what will happen later, right? You may hit traffic and your doctor's appointment might run over. Or, you might find the roads are clear and your appointment only lasted 15 minutes instead of the scheduled 30 minutes. In other words, you just don't know. The only thing you do know for sure is that you are in this office right now, and at the moment you are not late for anything. So, the only thing that is different about worrying about the future as opposed to paying attention to the present moment is that one makes you really anxious and the other makes you less anxious. How does worrying about being late later this afternoon make you feel physically?

P: Agitated, tense, stressed out!

T: And what about the thought that you are not late right now?

P: Well, a little less tense.

T: So, sitting still and observing your experience in the present moment doesn't mean trying to pretend you are not worried about what is going to happen later in the day, or trying not to think about memories from the past. Instead, sitting still and observing your experience means noticing in an objective, curious way that your thoughts are focused on potential negative events that may or may not happen in the future, and noticing that these thoughts also make you feel tense and anxious, and cause you to feel like fidgeting in your seat. Observing these reactions as they are happening in the present moment allows you to take in other, important information that is happening in the here and now that you might have otherwise missed. Noting to yourself in a curious way, "Huh, that's interesting. When I stop moving, my thoughts wander toward worries about being late and something bad happening. When I think these thoughts my muscles tense up. When I shift my focus to the room, my thoughts are that I am here now, and not late. When I think these thoughts my muscles relax a little." Refocusing your attention from the future to the present allows you to start understanding your reactions better, and to see where your interacting thoughts, feelings, and behaviors might be making the situation worse.

Case Vignette #3

In the following case vignette, the therapist is explaining to the patient that although present-focused awareness is a difficult skill to acquire, it gets easier over time with practice.

P: I don't think I'm doing this right. I can't focus, and I can't stop thinking about things.

T: There is no right or wrong way to practice present-focused awareness. This is a skill you might be learning for the first time. We are not used to just noticing our experience, we are used to being right in the "middle" of our experience. So, as with anything you are learning for the first time, expecting yourself to be able to do it "perfectly" from the start is not realistic. The first time you rode a bike did you just jump on and peddle off into the sunset? Or did you fall off, maybe even several times, before you found your balance? The same holds true for practicing observing your experience in this way. You might find your thoughts carry you away a hundred times, but you can also "get back on the bike" a hundred times by refocusing your attention every time you notice your thoughts carrying you away, until eventually it gets easier to stay on. And, the very fact that you notice yourself getting carried off by your thoughts means you *are* successfully observing your experience!

Case Vignette #4

In the following case vignette, the therapist is explaining to the patient the importance of practicing the exercises in this chapter.

P: I don't have time to meditate.

T: It can be very difficult in the midst of everything you have to juggle to add "one more thing." What we are talking about here, however, is committing to practicing for at least one week, taking 10, 15 minutes out of your day, once in the morning, and once in the afternoon or evening, to try and practice this skill. That might mean that for one week you set the alarm clock 15 minutes early. Or you put the kids to bed 15 minutes earlier, or you start dinner 15 minutes later.

P: But I'm not sure doing that will really help. I'm so busy as it is. Is it really necessary to do it every day?

T: What you gain by committing to practice for one week is an opportunity to get more comfortable with the experience of shifting your attention from being "stuck in your head" to observing your experience in an objective way, something you can continue to practice informally throughout the day using the Anchoring in the Present exercises. This will be an important skill that, over time and with practice, will start to become more automatic, allowing you to start to see where your reactions to your emotions may be adding to your distress and break the cycle before it starts. Remember, this is a new, probably very weak, muscle that needs exercising. You are not expected to master this in a week, just give yourself the opportunity to experience what it might be like to observe your experience instead of be caught up in the middle of it. Once you have allowed yourself to formally practice for at least a week, you can decide whether you want to make formal practice a regular part of your day. In any case, it will help you to get your informal practice underway.

Managing Problems

Some patients may be resistant to the idea of mindful awareness, finding it difficult, or even "hokey," as illustrated in Case Vignette #1. Others may feel that by simply observing their experience they are not "doing enough" to address their symptoms, and this may seem inherently unsatisfying to them. It is important in any case to convey to patients the rationale behind practicing present-focused awareness, and to be sure patients fully understand this rationale. Practicing present-focused, mindful awareness in this program is viewed as an important skill that will enhance the patient's ability to proceed through the remainder of treatment. It is viewed as an attentional shift that allows patients to step out of their experience, enabling them to identify where specific thoughts, physical sensations, and/or behaviors may be leading them astray.

It can be helpful to use the Three-Component Model of Emotions form to demonstrate how emotional experiences emerge as a dynamic, interacting cycle of thoughts, physical sensations, and behaviors, each of which influence and "feed off" of the other. Have patients give examples from their recent experiences, and draw arrows demonstrating how each domain is influencing the others. Explain to patients that most of the time we exist right in the middle of this chaos. This makes it very difficult to find an adaptive way to cope in response. Practicing present-focused awareness enables us to step outside of this chaos, allowing us to adopt a more objective view of it. You might demonstrate this by drawing a larger circle around all three domains, demonstrating where the patient's focus ought to be, observing this interaction as a whole from a distance, rather than being stuck in the middle of it. From this objective distance, patients will be better able to identify where they might intervene to break the cycle. For example, by stepping back and observing their experience, patients may be able to recognize how a catastrophic thought leads to heightened autonomic arousal, which may fuel further catastrophic thoughts, causing them to engage in escape or avoidance. Specifically, we instruct patients to use their breath or other chosen cue to anchor them in the present, followed by a quick "three-point check," observing their current thoughts, physical sensations, and behaviors, and identifying anything that is occurring within these three domains that may be serving to increase their distress. As such, present-focused, mindful awareness is an important first step in breaking maladaptive cycles of responding.

Homework

 Instruct the patient to continue monitoring progress by completing the OASIS and ODSIS forms and charting the Progress Record.

Instruct the patient to continue using the Monitoring Emotions and EDBs in Context form to identify emotional triggers and responses to these triggers.

Have the patient set aside time to deliberately practice nonjudgmental present-focused awareness twice a day for at least a week using the exercise in Chapter 7 of the workbook. If a different exercise was chosen for the session, provide the patient with a copy of the exercise to use at home. The patient should record his or her experiences on the Nonjudgmental Present-Focused Emotion Awareness form.

✎ Subsequent to a period of deliberate practice, encourage the patient to informally practice present-focused awareness several times throughout the day, using his or her chosen cue, such as the breath, to help anchor to the present. Have the patient practice anchoring to the present once per day and record on the Anchoring in the Present form in Chapter 7 of the workbook.

✎ Ask the patient to choose at least two songs from his or her own music collection that have strong personal meaning or memories associated with them. Encourage the patient to use his or her chosen cue to help anchor to the present, particularly if the patient is getting "carried away" by his or her thoughts. Have the patient record reactions to the songs on the Mood Induction Recording Form in Chapter 7 of the workbook, so reactions can be discussed in the next session. Instruct the patient to perform this exercise multiple times on separate days and encourage the patient to notice how emotional reactions may differ, depending on how he or she was feeling beforehand. Also suggest the patient use the Three-Component Model of Emotions form to explore reactions further.

Chapter 9 | *Module 4: Cognitive Appraisal and Reappraisal*

(Corresponds to Chapter 8 of the workbook)

Materials Needed

■ Ambiguous picture for in-session exercise

■ Looking at Your Interpretations form

■ Downward Arrow Technique form

■ Identifying and Evaluating Automatic Appraisals form

Goals

■ Review homework from previous session

■ Explain the reciprocal relationship between thoughts and emotions

■ Introduce automatic appraisals

■ Introduce and help patient identify common thinking traps

■ Introduce and help patient practice cognitive reappraisal to increase flexibility in thinking

Summary of Information in Chapter 8 of UP Workbook

■ The nature of cognitive appraisal, including the reciprocal influence between thoughts and emotions.

■ Automatic appraisals and two common thinking traps that occur in the range of emotion disorders. The first is probability overestimation, where the likelihood of the feared outcome occurring is greatly exaggerated. The second is catastrophizing, where the aversiveness and consequences of the event are exaggerated and one's ability to cope with it is underestimated.

- The importance of flexibility in appraising situations is emphasized. These thinking traps are not "wrong" or "bad"; rather, they become problematic when they are applied rigidly and begin to occur automatically and indiscriminate of the context in which they occur.

- Cognitive reappraisal is offered as a way of increasing flexibility in appraising situations, not as a way of eliminating "bad" or "faulty" ways of thinking. Countering probability overestimation involves objectively evaluating the likelihood of the event actually occurring, based on previous experience. Decatastrophizing involves the reevaluation of the aversiveness of the consequences of the feared event, and an objective appraisal of one's ability to cope with the event if it does occur.

Key Concepts

The key concepts for this module include a discussion of cognitive appraisal and reappraisal. Patients are expected to develop a greater awareness of ways in which they interpret or appraise situations, and to learn how thoughts influence cycles of emotional responding. You will work with patients to help them develop a greater flexibility in thinking. In this section, the goals for the patient are to:

- Learn to identify maladaptive automatic appraisals.

- Learn to evaluate these appraisals and increase flexibility in thinking.

Homework Review

Begin with a review of the patient's OASIS, ODSIS, and Progress Record forms, as well as the Monitoring Emotions and EDBs in Context form. Patients will have completed the Nonjudgmental Present-Focused

Emotion Awareness, Mood Induction Recording, and Anchoring in the Present forms. You will want to review these forms with the patient and assess progress in the patient's ability to identify and objectively evaluate his or her emotional responses. Some patients will have difficulty beginning to take a more objective stance towards their emotions. It is also common for patients to report difficulty translating what they were able to do during the earlier formal practices (e.g., Nonjudgmental Present-Focused Emotion Awareness form) to more informal day-to-day situations (e.g., Anchoring in the Present Form). It is important to help patients recognize that the exercise is a means to an end, and the process is what they are practicing, not the exercise itself. Collectively, these homework forms are designed to help patients begin to take a more objective stance toward their emotions. The first step is helping patients practice what it feels like to bring themselves into the present moment using the formal practice of a preselected mindfulness exercise (Nonjudgmental Present-Focused Emotion Awareness form). This is typically a new experience, and can be difficult for patients to get the hang of, much like developing a sense of balance when learning to ride a bike for the first time. You can help the patient practice this skill by utilizing an in-session exercise where the patient engages in an everyday task (e.g., eating a snack) and focuses on the sensory experience of that task. This can help give the patient a better sense of how to complete this first step of the homework from Module 3.

Once the patient has developed a sense for what the process "feels like" it is time to begin practicing that process while doing everyday tasks, such as while eating dinner, washing the dishes, or even taking a walk (using the Anchoring in the Present form). This will help the process begin to feel more natural, and will ultimately help patients to apply this process in the context of an emotional response. The Mood Induction Recording Form is used to help patients begin to practice this process in the context of their own emotions. This is an important step for patients to begin to strengthen this objective response in the context of self-relevant emotional responses. When reviewing homework from Module 3 with patients, it is important to continually remind them that they are developing and strengthening a process, or a new way of responding when they notice themselves being pushed or pulled by the intensity of an emotional response. This skill will serve as a base for subsequent treatment components, so some patients will benefit from continuing this practice while you advance through subsequent treatment modules.

Introduction to Cognitive Appraisal

In explaining cognitive appraisal, the following points should be discussed:

1. First, it is important to introduce the idea that there are a large number of different aspects (or stimuli) that a person can attend to or focus on in any given situation. This is the way the human mind works—serving as a filter by focusing on certain aspects of a situation and assigning meaning to those aspects, in order to increase the efficiency and speed of response to a given situation. Experiences from the past also help us interpret or appraise current situations, and then these interpretations and appraisals are used to project what might happen in the future. It is important to convey that this often happens without awareness.

2. Which aspects of the situation we focus on helps to determine the kinds of emotions experienced in response to a given situation. The ambiguous picture exercise (presented next) can be used to help patients identify how their appraisals can influence their feeling or mood states. This can be accomplished by asking patients to describe how various appraisals would trigger certain feelings (e.g., *"How would/did interpretation X make you feel?"*). This portion of the exercise offers the therapist the opportunity to model nonjudgmental awareness and acceptance of feelings, by validating the patient's emotional reactions (e.g., *"Of course you would feel Y if you interpreted the situation that way. It is natural to feel Y if X were true"*).

3. It is just as important to illustrate how emotions can influence the kinds of appraisals that are made in a given situation. The ambiguous picture example can also help illustrate how feelings or mood states can influence appraisals. We have found it useful to ask patients to describe how moods or feelings might lead them to appraise the situation differently (e.g., *"If you felt Y, how do you think you would interpret that situation?"*). It can also be helpful to

have patients discuss how multiple emotions (i.e., fear, anxiety, sadness, and anger) might influence their appraisals. This portion of the exercise helps patients understand how their feelings or mood states can help determine how they appraise (or interpret) situations. This discussion often leads nicely into introducing the key concept of automatic appraisal to patients.

Demonstration of Cognitive Appraisal: Ambiguous Picture Exercise

The following in-session exercise may be used to show how many different appraisals of a situation are possible – and to note how these appraisals are affected by current mood. First, present the ambiguous picture (the picture is provided for the patient in Chapter 8 of the workbook). While viewing the image, the patient should spend some time considering different appraisals (or interpretations) about the picture. After approximately 30 seconds have elapsed, put the picture away and ask for the patient's initial appraisal of the ambiguous picture. After identifying the initial or automatic appraisal, assist with generation of alternative appraisals about what might be happening in the picture. Instruct the patient to record appraisals on the Looking at Your Interpretations form in Chapter 8 of the workbook.

Therapist Note:

■ *Encourage patients to generate as many alternate appraisals as possible, even if some seem less plausible. Some patients have difficulty generating alternate appraisals. Validate that this can be difficult at first, but that with practice it gets easier and can become "second nature." Emphasize that there is no right answer and that the purpose of the exercise is not to change appraisals so that they are more "appropriate" or "better." Nor is the purpose to come up with the "right" appraisal. Rather, the purpose is to illustrate that despite the speed with which we generate initial interpretations, other interpretations are possible.* ■

Automatic appraisals help us filter our experience and respond to situations quickly and efficiently. It is adaptive in some situations to focus on a few key salient pieces of information and exclude additional information or evidence. Over time, individuals often develop a particular way or style of appraising situations. Research has found that individuals with emotional disorders are more likely to latch onto negative, more pessimistic appraisals. It can be useful to use the patient's initial interpretation of the ambiguous picture to illustrate this point, or to refer back to the boss/teacher example in Chapter 8 of the workbook.

It is important to identify the core automatic appraisal that is driving the emotional response, not merely the surface level appraisals that are often more easily accessible. It can be helpful to use the downward arrow technique to help patients to identify their core appraisals. For example, if someone described avoiding a social encounter and the related appraisal was "I won't have anything to say to people," this would show a disconnect between the extreme behavior (avoidance) and the relatively mild automatic appraisal. What may be more likely is that the patient interpreted the situation as, "I won't have anything to say, people will reject me, and I will never have any friends for the rest of my life." The Downward Arrow Technique form in Chapter 8 of the workbook can be useful for helping patients to identify their core automatic appraisal by asking them questions such as "What would happen if this were true?" and "What would it mean about you if this were true (or if this did happen)?"

Latching onto a single appraisal (or type of appraisal) about a situation or event repeatedly can create a powerful heuristic, and start to exclude other ways of thinking about or interpreting a situation or event. Although filtering out unnecessary information is adaptive and helpful, it can become problematic when a person continues to filter out additional information and exclude other possible, more realistic appraisals of a situation. Such filtering may lead to increased negative emotions and, in turn, to more general core automatic appraisals (e.g., "I'll never do anything right," "I'm worthless," etc.). Thus, both automatic appraisals and emotions maintain this cycle—our appraisals influence how we feel, and our feelings influence the future appraisals we make.

Two common automatic appraisals or "thinking traps" often found among individuals with emotional disorders include *probability overestimation* (or *jumping to conclusions*) and *catastrophizing* (or *thinking the worst*). It can be helpful to use examples from the patient's homework (or daily life) to discuss thinking traps. Try to elicit specific examples of appraisals that may be rigid or problematic in that the appraisal focuses on one aspect or interpretation of a situation that may not be helpful in the long term. It is also useful to try and ascertain the automatic appraisals patients may have that are adaptive–ones that filter out truly unnecessary information and focus on motivating patients to deal with a specific problem or task. However, spend the most time discussing the types of appraisals that get in the way of functioning. Detailed information about thinking traps is included in the patient workbook.

Cognitive Reappraisal

Thinking traps maintain the problematic emotional response cycles by decreasing our flexibility in thinking, and preventing us from acknowledging a range of different interpretations or considering the context in which something occurs. The problem with these automatic appraisals is not that they are "bad" or "wrong" ways of thinking but that they are limiting, as they represent only one possible interpretation of the situation. Thus, the goal of cognitive reappraisal is to increase flexibility in appraising situations, *not* to replace bad thoughts or "fix" faulty ways of thinking.

One way out of these thinking traps is to pay attention to appraisals, and evaluate them not as "truths," but as possible interpretations of the situation. Instead of automatically thinking that the worst scenario is going to happen, it is important to begin to introduce and consider other interpretations. Thoughts about the worst scenario can still be there, but they can "coexist" with other possible assessments of the situation. The goal is to allow flexibility in our thoughts, and allow for alternate appraisals of emotionally provocative situations—appraisals that are anchored in the present situation and take the current context into consideration.

It is common for patients to judge or blame themselves for the automatic interpretations they make. This can create a barrier to generating flexibility in appraisals because the more patients blame themselves, the more negative affect they experience in response to the thoughts, and the more negative thoughts they have. It is important to help patients practice being aware of automatic appraisals in a nonjudgmental way, noticing the appraisal and allowing it to pass through their minds, rather than holding onto it as the *only* way of considering the situation and "running with" that interpretation. The point is to be aware of the thinking trap and, within the context of the emotion being experienced, consider the trap not as the only truth, but as one way of thinking about the situation. This will allow for increased flexibility in thinking.

Cognitive reappraisal is a useful skill for helping to break problematic emotional response cycles, and has been found to be an effective strategy for changing the way an emotion or event is experienced. Learning to generate more realistic and evidence-based interpretations of emotion-provoking situations facilitates emotion regulation.

Two reappraisal strategies are helpful in learning to reevaluate automatic appraisals and come up with alternative interpretations. They are: *countering probability overestimation* and *decatastrophizing*. It is especially important to be empathetic to both the scenario and the patient's emotional experience during this process. It is difficult to acknowledge some of the core fears that patients have been trying to avoid for a long time. The purpose of cognitive reappraisal is not to eliminate all thoughts related to negative appraisals, nor is it to "punish" patients for having negative interpretations. Cognitive reappraisal strategies are useful to help patients gain some perspective on thoughts, so that the negative, automatic thoughts do not further feed the problematic emotional response cycle. Reappraising automatic appraisals is also a helpful way to facilitate later emotion exposures, by allowing for different assessments of the emotions when they are experienced. Helping patients to practice realistically assessing their appraisals will provide some motivation when they are faced with completing a difficult emotion exposure. Cognitive reappraisal strategies are discussed in more detail in the patient workbook.

Case Vignettes

Case Vignette #1

In the following vignette, the patient is having difficulty identifying his thoughts.

P: I don't know. I didn't think anything. I mean, I just had to escape. I had to get out of there right away!

T: What do you remember thinking while you were standing in front of everyone?

P: I was thinking about the presentation I was supposed to give.

T: Were you making any specific predictions about how it might go? Or did you have any concerns about what might happen?

P: Well, I was pretty sure it was going to go badly, just like the last time I tried to give a presentation. I was really concerned that the audience would see how anxious I was, and think that I didn't know what I was talking about.

Case Vignette #2

In the following vignette, the therapist uses the downward arrow technique to help the patient identify the core appraisal that drove her to cancel her date.

P: So I cancelled the date that I had scheduled last week.

T: What happened?

P: I was getting ready to go on that blind date and I started getting really anxious.

T: What did you notice while you were getting ready for your date?

P: I noticed some of the usual physical symptoms, like increased heart rate and some sweating. I was worrying that I wouldn't have anything to say. I got so anxious that I just called and said that I was sorry, but I couldn't make it.

T: It sounds like you were quite anxious about not having anything to say during your date. I'm curious, what would happen (or what would it mean about you) if you didn't have anything to say?

P: Well, I guess if I didn't have anything to say, my date would think I am boring.

T: And what would happen if they thought you were boring?

P: I won't get invited on a second date.

T: Ok, so if this date thought you were boring and you weren't invited on a second date, what would happen next?

P: Then no one will want to date me and I would be alone forever.

Managing Problems

As illustrated in Case Vignette #1, some patients can have difficulty identifying their thoughts. Often times, these individuals will become so focused on the intensity of the emotion in the moment that they will effectively "ignore" the events or moments that preceded their reaction. In cases like these, it can be helpful to guide the patient "back in time" to before he or she entered the situation, or when he or she had just entered the situation, to help the patient begin to identify his or her automatic appraisals. In Case Vignette #1 the therapist helped the patient to identify what kinds of thoughts he was having prior to the situation (e.g., giving a presentation) and his response in the situation itself (e.g., intense urge to escape). In cases like this, patients will likely benefit from additional focus on, and practice with, identifying their automatic appraisals, before moving on to cognitive reappraisal.

Another potential roadblock that can arise while administering the interventions presented in this chapter is when the patient identifies an appraisal, but there is a noticeable disconnect between the nature of the appraisal and the intensity of the patient's response in that situation. The disconnect between the patient's behavior and his or her appraisal of the situation is a cue that the patient has not identified his or her core automatic appraisal. As illustrated in Case Vignette #2, the therapist used the downward arrow technique to identify the core appraisal that was driving the patient's emotional response in that situation (e.g., calling to cancel the date). It is essential to identify this core appraisal to maximize the benefit of cognitive reappraisal. The Downward Arrow Technique form is useful for helping patients to understand this disconnect.

Sometimes, individuals experiencing intrusive cognitions (e.g., obsessions or worry) will become so fixated on evaluating the *actual* probability of the event occurring that this itself can become a form of cognitive avoidance. In these cases, it is helpful to redirect the patients away from evaluating probabilities to evaluating their ability to cope with the consequences, and the meaning they are ascribing to the event if it were to happen. In addition to redirecting these individuals to evaluate the consequences associated with the feared event itself, it can also be useful to establish a time limit for patients to use the reappraisal skill to help ensure they don't get stuck in a cognitive avoidance cycle.

Homework

✎ Instruct the patient to continue monitoring progress by completing the OASIS and ODSIS forms and charting the Progress Record.

✎ Ask the patient to try using the Downward Arrow Technique form in Chapter 8 of the workbook to identify core automatic appraisals from previous homework forms (e.g., the Monitoring Emotions and EDBs in Context form).

✎ Have the patient use the Identifying and Evaluating Automatic Appraisals form to monitor appraisals and emotions. Instruct the patient to fill in the first four columns only (the situation or trigger, the automatic appraisal, the emotion, and the identified thinking trap).

✎ Once the patient has identified automatic appraisals, he or she should begin the reappraisal process—if you feel the patient is ready (see Therapist Note below). Instruct the patient to generate at least one alternative appraisal for every automatic appraisal (although generating more than one alternative can be helpful, as well) and write it down in the last column of the Identifying and

Evaluating Automatic Appraisals form. Remind the patient that the goal is not to entirely believe a new interpretation, but rather to allow it to coexist with the automatic negative appraisal. Neither of the interpretations is necessarily correct – they are each examples of a range of possible interpretations.

Therapist Note:

▪ *Some patients require more practice with cognitive appraisal than others, and it may take longer to address all material in one session. Therefore you may elect to assign the first four columns of the Identifying and Evaluating Automatic Appraisals form after one session, and subsequently assign cognitive reappraisal (the final column) the following session. For patients who are able to grasp the concepts in one session you should feel free to assign the full Identifying and Evaluating Automatic Appraisals form.* ▪

✎ You may also have the patient continue practicing skills introduced in previous modules. For example, it can be helpful for patients who have completed Chapter 7 of the workbook to continue practicing present-focused awareness using the Anchoring in the Present form. While the main focus of the homework should be practicing the skills learned in this chapter, you should feel free to assign one or two worksheets from the previous chapters, if extra practice would be of benefit.

Chapter 10 *Module 5: Emotion Avoidance*

(Corresponds to Chapter 9 of the workbook)

Materials Needed

- List of Emotion Avoidance Strategies form

Goals

- Review homework from previous session

- Introduce concept of emotion avoidance

- Present several types of emotion avoidance strategies and discuss how these strategies contribute to the negative cycle of emotional responding

- Help the patient identify his or her own emotion avoidance strategies

- Demonstrate the paradoxical effects of emotion avoidance

Summary of Information in Chapter 9 of UP Workbook

- Emotion avoidance refers to any strategies someone might use to avoid feeling strong emotions, or to prevent emotions from becoming more intense.

- Emotion avoidance most often occurs with regard to negative emotions, but can occur for positive emotions as well.

- Although emotion avoidance strategies may be useful in some situations, they rarely work well in the long term.

- In addition to more "obvious" avoidance, such as when someone refuses to enter a situation that is likely to produce emotional distress, avoidance strategies can be broken down into three main types: subtle behavioral avoidance, cognitive avoidance, and the use of "safety signals."

- Attempts to avoid emotions are generally unsuccessful, and are likely to paradoxically increase the frequency and intensity of the very thoughts and emotions the individual is trying to suppress.

Key Concepts

In this chapter, the concept of emotion avoidance is introduced. As previously noted, *emotion avoidance* refers to any strategies one might use to avoid feeling strong emotions, or to prevent emotions from becoming more intense. You will work collaboratively with the patient to identify these strategies. Emotion avoidance can also be demonstrated in-session to help patients gain a greater understanding of this concept. In this section, the goal for the patient is to:

- Identify patterns of emotion avoidance and gain an understanding of how emotion avoidance strategies contribute to the development and maintenance of negative emotions.

Homework Review

As with prior chapters, begin with a review of the patient's OASIS, ODSIS, and Progress Record forms, as well as any additional forms that may have been assigned from prior sessions. Patients also will have completed the Downward Arrow Technique form, as well as the Identifying and Evaluating Automatic Appraisals form. You will want to review these forms with the patient and assess progress in the patient's ability to identify core cognitions and evaluate their anxious and negative thoughts. Some patients will have difficulty identifying their automatic appraisals, and may need some assistance in completing this task. Further, patients may also report difficulty identifying appraisals and using reappraisal strategies at the time when they are experiencing strong emotions. This is quite common. However, it is important for patients to recognize that some level of cognitive processing is occurring, even if it is outside their immediate level of awareness. The homework is designed to help patients gain awareness of their thoughts, and patients may find that increasing awareness will, in and of itself, help "slow down" the emotional response and provide them with greater opportunity to alter their emotional experience. It takes time to develop the ability to catch a thought "in flight," and patients should not expect that they will master this skill in a short period of time. Initially, patients may find it easier to identify and evaluate automatic appraisals before and after, as opposed to during, an emotional response. Practicing the skill in this way can still be a useful means of altering emotion, and will help patients build greater awareness of their thoughts as one of the three essential components of the emotional experience. Over time, patients will likely find it easier to identify their thoughts as the emotional response unfolds.

Introduction to Emotion Avoidance

Descriptions of several types of emotion avoidance strategies, including subtle behavioral avoidance, cognitive avoidance, and safety signals, are provided in Chapter 9 of the workbook to assist patients with identifying the various ways in which they may attempt to avoid their emotions. In addition to these emotion avoidance strategies, you should also be aware of the potential avoidance of somatic sensations associated with emotions. This is quite common across emotional disorders, since these sensations may trigger intense affect. Also, it is important to note that emotion avoidance can occur for positive as well as negative emotions. For instance, patients suffering from depression often report difficulty in allowing themselves to feel positive emotions. For these individuals, treatment may involve reducing avoidance of positive emotions by promoting activities that provide opportunity for positive reinforcement, and which may foster a greater sense of efficacy. Asking patients to fully engage in these activities, and to "embrace" the positive emotions that occur, is essential to changing the emotional response.

Note that the types of avoidance identified by patients may differ depending on the presenting emotional disorder. So, for instance, patients experiencing symptoms of panic and agoraphobic avoidance may be more likely to identify the use of safety signals as a means of avoiding their emotions than, say, a patient with symptoms of social phobia—and, in some cases, a combination of subtle behavioral avoidance and cognitive avoidance may become sufficiently extensive to produce emotional numbing. It is not essential for patients to identify all types of emotion avoidance. However, you should work with the patient to develop a comprehensive list of emotional avoidance strategies that can then be modified as treatment progresses. Examples of emotion avoidance strategies, and the disorder with which they are most often associated, are presented in Table 10.1.

It is important for patients to understand that engaging in avoidance can contribute to the maintenance of current patterns of emotional responding. While patients may find avoidance strategies useful in some situations, as they tend to inhibit their experience of intense emotions in the short term, they rarely work well in the long term. First, avoidance prevents *habituation*, or a reduction in response strength with repeated presentations of the feared stimulus. Second, and more importantly, avoidance interferes with a process of *extinction*, or a decrement in responding through repetition of unreinforced responding: repeated encounters with feared stimulus without aversive consequences. Avoidance also prevents patients from developing a sense of control or efficacy in

Table 10.1 Emotion Avoidance Strategies and Their Associated Disorders

Emotion-Avoidance Strategy	Disorder Most Often Associated
Subtle behavioral avoidance	
Avoiding eye contact	Social phobia
Avoiding drinking caffeine	Panic disorder with or without agoraphobia (PDA)
Attempting to control breathing	PDA
Avoiding exercise and other forms of physiological arousal (interoceptive avoidance)	PDA/Depression
Avoiding touching sink/toilet	Obsessive-compulsive disorder (OCD)
Procrastination (avoiding emotionally salient tasks)	Generalized anxiety disorder (GAD)

Table 10.1 (Continued)

Emotion-Avoidance Strategy	Disorder Most Often Associated
Cognitive avoidance	
Distraction (reading a book, watching television)	Depression/PDA
"Tuning out" during a conversation	Social phobia
Reassuring self that everything is okay	GAD
Trying to prevent thoughts from coming into mind	OCD
Distraction from reminders of trauma	Post-traumatic stress disorder
Forcing self to "think positive"	Depression
Worrying	GAD
Rumination	Depression
Thought suppression	All disorders
Safety signals	
Carrying a cell phone	PDA/GAD
Carrying empty medication bottles	PDA
Holding onto "good luck" charms	OCD
Carrying mace at all times	PTSD
Carrying a water bottle	PDA
Having reading material/prayer books on hand	GAD
Carrying sunglasses or items to hide face/eyes	Social phobia

managing the feared outcome. Finally, it prohibits patients from challenging existing beliefs and developing more rational beliefs regarding the feared situation, including their ability to tolerate negative emotions.

Demonstration of Emotion Avoidance

In Chapter 9 of the workbook, two specific in-session exercises are provided to demonstrate how emotion avoidance often backfires, such as when patients are trying not to think about something important or distressing. These exercises can help patients gain a greater conceptual understanding of emotion avoidance, and allow them to see how these strategies work (and don't work) with regard to their emotions. While we find both exercises useful in helping patients to understand the concept of emotion avoidance, you may wish to develop additional exercises as well.

The first in-session exercise described in the workbook is adapted from an experiment conducted by Professors Daniel Wegner and David Schneider on mental control and thought suppression (Wegner, Schneider, Carter, & White, 1987). In the second exercise, the imaginal exposure, patients are asked to try not to think about a situation or a memory that is particularly emotional for them.

We have found these exercises helpful in illustrating the idea that attempts to suppress thoughts (and emotions) are generally unsuccessful. In fact, suppression may actually increase the frequency and intensity of the very thoughts and emotions the individual is trying to stop. You may wish to point out to patients that while they may have been able to avoid thinking about the memory or situation for at least a period of time, to be sure they were not thinking of the memory (which was the purpose of the task), they would need to occasionally "check" to make sure thoughts about the memory or situation were not in their mind. This very process then involves thinking about the memory or situation, and thus ensures they will have to think about it at some level.

Setting the Stage

One of the primary goals of treatment is to help patients learn to face negative emotions, and the situations that elicit them, without engaging in any forms of avoidance. The material covered in this chapter is important for helping patients engage in more difficult emotion exposure exercises later in treatment. In order for patients to fully engage in these exercises, they must be aware of, and subsequently reduce or prevent, any attempts to disengage from the situation or diminish their emotional response.

Case Vignette #1

In the following vignette, the therapist is helping the patient understand the concept of emotion avoidance.

P: If I know that avoiding is bad, and serves to maintain my fear, why do I keep doing it?

T: We believe that avoidance is maintained through a process of reinforcement. When we do something that prevents the presentation of an aversive stimulus, the behavior is strengthened or reinforced. This can, of course, occur for both internal stimuli, such as physical feelings, thoughts, or even emotions, as well as for external stimuli, such as specific situations or objects that are threatening.

P: But what causes the avoidance behavior?

T: It really differs from situation to situation, but usually there's a trigger that signals the possible occurrence of an aversive stimulus. Once this trigger is present, we're much more likely to avoid. It's just something we learn to do. It serves an adaptive function, really.

P: I guess that's the downside of being so smart, and learning to adapt to things around us.

Case Vignette #2

In the following vignette, the therapist is working with the patient to define what constitutes adaptive versus non-adaptive avoidance behaviors.

P: Typically, when I get ready for a presentation, I spend a lot of time preparing. I guess I'm avoiding the possibility of making a mistake. But isn't that a good thing? I mean, I know a lot of people who do that. Maybe my anxiety is actually helping me here. I just want to do a good job.

T: That's a really good point. I agree that avoidance can sometimes be adaptive, and I can see why you might not want to make too many mistakes during an important talk. But do you think that the amount you prepare is reasonable, given the importance of the talks? After the talk is over, do you look back and wonder whether you needed to prepare as much as you did?

P: I see where you're coming from. I guess I probably don't need to prepare as much as I do. Usually the talks are pretty unimportant, but I feel like I prepare for everything the same way. And even for the important talks, I tend to go a little overboard.

T: Do you have a sense of why you prepare so much?

P: Like we talked about last week, I guess I get worried about doing a good job. I get scared that I'll get anxious, my mind will go blank, and I won't be able to continue.

T: I think we can agree that going into a big talk without any preparation at all is probably not the best strategy. But at this point, it seems like the function of your behavior is primarily to avoid an outcome which is not likely to occur. That is, I think you over-prepare in order to avoid feeling anxious in that situation. You're afraid that your anxiety will significantly interfere with your performance.

P: I would agree with that.

T: But I'm not sure you have much data to support that idea. You said yourself that even when you get anxious during a talk, you still do well. And last week we also agreed that even if you didn't do a good job, it would be fine in the end…that you would be able to handle it. So in this situation, I feel like the over-preparing is not very adaptive for you. In fact, I think it prevents you from challenging some of the ideas you have about experiencing anxiety in that situation. That's not going to make that situation any easier in the future.

P: Good point doc. Maybe I should only prepare when the talk is really important and even then, I could try to keep it more reasonable. There's a part of me that knows I would do just fine, even if I didn't prepare.

Case Vignette #3

In the following vignette, the therapist helps the patient to see that she is engaging in emotion avoidance when she doesn't allow her husband to open their bedroom windows.

P: Last night it was really hot outside and my husband wanted to open the windows in our bedroom. He got upset with me because I wouldn't let him.

T: Why didn't you want to open the windows?

P: The noises outside can really disrupt my sleep. In the morning, the birds are always chirping. Sometimes they wake me up.

T: That seems reasonable. I wonder why your husband got so upset.

P: He thinks it's related to my anxiety. He says I'm paranoid.

T: I wonder why he thinks you're being paranoid.

P: Remember I told you that a couple of years ago our apartment got broken into? Well, after that, I got really anxious about someone breaking in again, especially at night. Since then, I haven't really wanted to leave the windows open.

T: So you lock your windows at night to prevent someone from breaking in while you and your husband are sleeping?

P: Not just because of that, but…yeah, I guess so. I know it's not very likely. We live on the third floor. But I get so anxious when we leave them open at night. I really have trouble sleeping.

T: It's hard to know sometimes whether we're engaging in a behavior out of personal preference, and when it might actually be an example of emotion avoidance. How do you think we might tease that out in this situation?

P: Well, I guess I wasn't too concerned about locking the window at night before the house was broken into. And when I'm at other people's houses, I'm much less concerned about it, even though the noise outside is pretty similar. So I guess maybe I'm avoiding the possibility of someone breaking into our house again even though it's unlikely to happen.

Managing Problems

Patients are typically able to identify when patterns of avoidance have become problematic. However, avoidance of threatening situations can sometimes be adaptive, and serves an important function for survival.

Some patients find this confusing, and may struggle with differentiating when, and under what circumstances, avoidance can be adaptive. So, as reflected in Case Vignette #2, the therapist will most likely find it beneficial to work with the patient to collaboratively define what constitutes adaptive versus non-adaptive avoidance behaviors, taking into consideration the patient's expectations of his own behavior, the specific context in which the behavior occurs, and the consequences with which it is associated. The ability to recognize when, and under what circumstances, a behavior should be considered adaptive or non-adaptive is essential to behavioral change, and helping patients develop this discrimination can be an important part of treatment.

Occasionally, patients may have difficulty identifying patterns of avoidance. The therapist should work collaboratively with the patient to identify problematic behaviors and then consider the function of these behaviors with regards to the patient's emotions. Possible patterns of avoidance can also be generated from the patient's diagnostic presentation, or by reflecting upon current functional impairment.

Also, as reflected in Case Vignette #3, some patients may have difficulty recognizing a behavior as avoidance, even though this may appear to be the case. For instance, a patient suffering from recurrent panic attacks may claim that they do not like the taste of coffee or never cared for amusement rides. While the patient may see those behaviors as simply reflecting personal preferences, as opposed to avoidance, the therapist should once again work with the patient to respectfully consider the possibility that these "preferences" may in fact reflect an underlying fear of internal or external stimuli.

Homework

✎ Instruct the patient to continue monitoring progress by completing the OASIS and ODSIS forms and charting the Progress Record.

✎ Have the patient complete the List of Emotion Avoidance Strategies form in Chapter 9 of the workbook. This form contains three columns that relate to the three types of strategies discussed in session (subtle behavioral avoidance, cognitive avoidance, and safety signals). In order to illustrate how to complete this form, you may wish to explain what each column represents and demonstrate how to fill in each column using some examples from the patient's experience (e.g., "You said you often distract yourself from focusing on panic sensations by having the window in the car down – that's an example of subtle behavioral avoidance. When you take your "lucky" keychain with you to make you feel better, that's an example of a safety signal").

Chapter 11 *Module 5: Emotion-Driven Behaviors*

(Corresponds to Chapter 10 of the workbook)

Materials Needed

- Changing EDBs form

Goals

- Review homework from previous session

- Reintroduce, and discuss in more depth, the concept of emotion-driven behaviors (EDBs)

- Introduce rationale for countering EDBs

- Identify maladaptive EDBs and develop alternative action tendencies

Summary of Information in Chapter 10 of UP Workbook

- Emotions tell us to act in a certain ways, or drive certain behaviors. These emotion-driven behaviors (EDBs) are adaptive and serve an important survival function. However, some EDBs may be less adaptive, or even harmful in managing a particular situation, depending on the context in which they occur.

- EDBs are different from emotion avoidance, in that EDBs tend to happen in response to an emotion that has been triggered, whereas avoidance strategies tend to happen *before* an emotion has even had a chance to occur.

- EDBs may reduce distressing emotions in the short term, but don't always work well in the long term and can actually contribute to the negative cycle of emotions.

- Patients should practice adopting behaviors that promote a pattern of approach, as opposed to avoidance, with regards to intense emotions.

- One of the most effective ways to break the cycle of emotions, and actually change the way emotions are experienced, is to adopt alternative behaviors.

Key Concepts

In this chapter, the concept of EDBs will be examined in greater detail. Patients will come to appreciate how EDBs can influence emotional experiences and contribute to the negative cycle of emotions. Patients will also learn to identify maladaptive EDBs and then work to counter these behaviors. In this section, the goals for the patient are to:

- Learn about emotion-driven behaviors (EDBs) and how they influence emotional experiences.

- Learn to identify and counter maladaptive EDBs.

Homework Review

Begin with a review of the patient's OASIS, ODSIS, and Progress Record forms, as well as any additional forms that may have been assigned from prior sessions. Next, review the patient's List of Emotion Avoidance Strategies form. You may find it useful to spend time discussing when, and under what circumstances, these avoidance strategies are most likely to occur. If the patient was unable to identify many specific avoidance strategies, assist him or her in this task. You may find it useful to refer back to the presenting symptoms identified during the initial assessment to help generate possible emotion avoidance strategies.

Reintroduction to Emotion-Driven Behaviors

In reintroducing the concept of emotion-driven behaviors (EDBs), which was first discussed in Chapter 5 of the workbook, you should address several important points as described in the sections that follow.

Adaptive versus Non-adaptive EDBs

One of the important functions of emotion is to direct an organism toward a specific set of behaviors that would be most adaptive to the situation at hand. For example, if a situation elicits anger, the emotion would motivate us to engage in angry behaviors, including verbal threats, physical attack, or a facial or bodily threat display. These behaviors generally serve an adaptive function, allowing us to respond quickly to our environment. However, they can also become maladaptive and contribute to the development and maintenance of disordered emotion. In other words, the same behaviors can be adaptive under some circumstances or in some contexts, but less adaptive in others. For example, a threatening situation might elicit anger and fear, which would, in turn, motivate us to engage in behaviors that were designed to be protective. In this case, feelings of anger and fear might elicit behaviors linked to the act of fighting, fleeing, or both. These behaviors would be entirely adaptive if, for instance, there was a threat present that could objectively result in a considerable degree of harm (e.g., we were about to be mugged). However, if a true threat was not present, and we were in fact experiencing a "false alarm," then the subsequent behaviors elicited by the emotions would likely be less adaptive in that particular situation.

You will most likely find it beneficial to collaboratively define what constitutes an adaptive versus non-adaptive behavior, taking into consideration the patient's expectations of his or her own behavior, the specific context in which the behavior occurs, and the consequences with which it is associated.

How EDBs are Established and Maintained

As discussed earlier in the treatment, EDBs are generally believed to be maintained or strengthened by a process of negative reinforcement, even if they are inappropriate to the situation. You might recall that a similar process was used in explaining maintenance of avoidance behaviors. Similar to emotion avoidance, patients have learned that engaging in certain behaviors eliminates or reduces the intensity of an aversive stimulus, whether it is internal or external in nature. As a result, the frequency of the behaviors increases over time. In fact, it might be helpful to remind the patient that this entire learning process serves an adaptive function, as it helps to protect the organism from harm. Unfortunately, however, patients have learned to respond in certain ways to stimuli that are, in fact, not actually threatening, and, as such, the behaviors do not truly serve an adaptive function. Discussing how EDBs become established and are maintained can often help patients alter their perspective on these behaviors and provide hope regarding their ability to change. Patients come to appreciate the possibility that new and more adaptive responses can also be learned.

Eliciting Personally Relevant Examples of EDBs

Examples of EDBs are presented in the workbook and in Table 11.1. You may find it useful to review these examples with the patient in order to generate additional discussion about EDBs, and to elicit examples that may be more personally relevant. In order for patients to eventually change their EDBs, first they need to identify them. Taking the time to help patients identify their EDBs is important to helping them change these behaviors as treatment progresses.

Consequences of Non-adaptive Coping

You will want to highlight the relationship between the behaviors and the emotions the patient is experiencing. You may find it useful to select an example from the patient's own life, and help him or her clearly map out (using a whiteboard or piece of paper) how engaging in EDBs makes

Table 11.1 Emotion-Driven Behaviors (EDBs), Their Associated Disorders, and Alternative Behaviors

EDB(s)	Disorder Most Often Associated	Alternative Behaviors
Calling relatives to check on safety	Generalized anxiety disorder (GAD)	Restricting contact/calling relatives
Perfectionistic behavior at work or home	Generalized anxiety disorder (GAD)	Leaving things untidy or unfinished
Checking locks, stove, or other appliances	Obsessive-compulsive disorder (OCD)	Repeatedly locking/unlocking and turning on/off until memory is unclear
Leaving (escaping from) a theater, religious service, or other crowded area	Panic disorder with agoraphobia (PDA)	Move to the center of the crowd; smile or produce non-fearful facial expressions
Social withdrawal	Depression	Behavioral activation
Leaving (escaping) a social situation	Social phobia	Staying in situation and approaching people
Verbally/physically attacking someone when in an argument	Post-traumatic stress disorder (PTSD)	Remove self from situation and/or practice relaxation techniques
Hypervigilance	All disorders	Focus attention on specific task at hand; meditation; relaxation

the patient feel. Usually engaging in EDBs makes the patient feel better for a short time (e.g., escaping from a situation that has triggered a panic attack); however, over time, engaging in these behaviors can actually make the patient feel *more* anxious (e.g., now that situation, and likely many others, begins to trigger anxiety). Return to the three-component model to assist the patient in understanding the role of EDBs in contributing to the emotional response.

In the end, patients should come to understand both the short- and long-term consequences of engaging in EDBs. Again, while engaging in an EDB might result in a short-term reduction of emotion, these behaviors can also contribute to the maintenance of the very emotions that the patient is trying to change. This idea is important with regard to treatment, and provides justification for the therapeutic procedure outlined in the following section.

Countering Patterns of Avoidance and EDBs

Identifying patterns of avoidance, as described in the previous chapter, and EDBs will assist the patient in targeting specific behaviors he or she would like to change during the course of treatment. Once the patient has a good understanding of these concepts, and is able to identify his or her own patterns of avoidance and EDBs, the patient will be able to work toward countering these behaviors. Review the following two primary therapeutic strategies:

1. Patients are instructed to begin engaging in activities and situations that are likely to evoke the emotions they are currently avoiding. This extends into the exposure exercises that occur more systematically as treatment progresses.

2. Patients will work toward counteracting maladaptive EDBs by developing and engaging in behaviors that run counter to these responses. In other words, patients will work toward acting in an alternative way from the EDB. For example, if a patient experiencing sadness and depression identifies withdrawal and activity reduction as EDBs, in order to *act alternatively* he or she might increase physical activity and engage more in rewarding activities.

You may wish to work with the patient on identifying EDBs and alternative behaviors. Examples of EDBs, the disorders with which they are most often associated, and alternative behaviors are presented in Table 11.1.

While these change strategies are relatively easy for patients to understand, implementing them on a consistent basis can be much more difficult. During the remainder of treatment, you will work with patients on challenging avoidance behaviors and implementing new, alternative actions.

The Changing EDBs form in Chapter 10 of the workbook is designed to assist patients with tracking and altering EDBs.

Case Vignettes

Case Vignette #1

In the following case vignette, the therapist is explaining to the patient the difference between emotion avoidance and EDBs.

P: I'm a little confused about the difference between emotion avoidance and EDBs. It all sounds like avoidance to me. What is the major distinction between the two?

T: Emotion avoidance is different from EDBs in that avoidance strategies tend to happen *before* an emotion has a chance to occur, whereas EDBs tend to happen in response to an emotion that has already been triggered. However, like EDBs, emotional avoidance strategies can also become powerful habits in maintaining the cycle of emotions.

Case Vignette #2

In the following case vignette, the therapist is reviewing EDBs and how they come about.

P: How did my EDBs get established in the first place?

T: That's a good question. First, EDBs are part of our emotions, so, in a sense, we're born with them. Whenever fear occurs in any species, not just humans, the tendency is to escape and run away. For anger, the EDB is to attack. Do you remember back in the beginning of treatment we talked a little bit about negative reinforcement? You probably learned that when you're feeling anxious at parties, escaping the situation tends to make you feel a lot better. That is, it produces a sudden reduction in your anxiety. And since you're concerned that other people can see when you're anxious and judge you negatively as a result, it's likely that the escape behavior was negatively reinforced, simply because it diminished your anxiety...it reduced something that was making you feel bad.

Because it was reinforced, it's likely to occur again in the future, especially the next time you're feeling anxious, even though there's nothing to be fearful about.

Case Vignette #3

In the following case vignette, the therapist works with the patient to help her distinguish between adaptive and maladaptive EDBs.

P: One of the hardest things for me is to be able to determine when an EDB is adaptive and when it's not. The other day, someone I know was making fun of me at work. It hurt my feelings and I got really upset. I wanted to say something, but instead I just got up and walked away.

T: What would you normally do in that situation?

P: Well, in the past, I've become really confrontational. I get upset. I mean, I go from zero to sixty. Once I get pushed past a certain point...it's not good...I can't calm down. Usually, I just blow up...sometimes I cry... sometimes both.

T: And what happened this time? When you walked away?

P: After a little while I started to calm down. I still felt bad, but I decided that maybe she didn't mean what she said, or that I just took it the wrong way. I have a tendency to do that sometimes. I still think she could've been a little nicer, though.

T: It seems that walking away actually gave you an opportunity to process the situation a little more.

P: Yes, but I don't want to be a doormat or anything. I still want to stand up for myself. Initially, when I walked away, I sort of felt like I might be avoiding my anger...like I was just escaping the situation.

T: I actually think you did a good job of engaging in an alternative behavior like we had talked about. Instead of getting locked into the same old response, you gave yourself a moment to look at your thoughts, and to process how you were feeling, which seems to have been pretty effective in reducing your initial anger, or at least it brought it to a different level. I can understand your concern about being a doormat, though. I wonder if you could have done anything else in that situation…maybe after you calmed down?

P: I thought about speaking with her after the fact. I was going to tell her that what she said hurt my feelings and made me upset. But then I got concerned she might think I was being stupid. Also, I was worried I might just get angry again and be unable to control it.

T: Now *that* sounds much more like avoidance. It sounds like speaking with your coworker about this situation after some of the initial anger had subsided may have been the way to go.

Managing Problems

As described in Case Vignette #1, some patients may struggle with understanding the distinction between avoidance and EDBs. The distinction may not be entirely crucial in a practical sense, as patients will more generally work toward challenging maladaptive patterns of responding (which includes both emotional avoidance and EDBs). Theoretically, however, we view the difference between emotional avoidance and EDBs as being more temporal in nature and it can be described as such. With that said, you may still sometimes find it difficult to help patients distinguish between the two. Again, it is more important for patients to recognize maladaptive patterns of responding with regards to their emotions, rather than become 100% accurate in classifying these responses. You may choose to help the patient gain a broader understanding of why both avoidance and EDBs can be problematic, and how altering these response patterns is essential to therapeutic change.

EDBs can sometimes be difficult for patients to identify. Several tracking forms have been developed to assist patients in becoming better at identifying EDBs. In addition, you may want to revisit some of the emotional tracking exercises the patients completed in prior weeks to generate examples, or to help the patient identify common EDBs associated with their emotions.

Depending on the presenting symptoms, the Changing EDBs form may not always be entirely sufficient for tracking and modifying these behaviors. For instance, for patients presenting with more compulsive behaviors, such as repeated checking or handwashing, tracking the behaviors using the form may become too tedious, which could then affect compliance. In response, you may wish to use an alternative method of tracking these behaviors, such as a frequency counter. As long as the patient has a good understanding of the behavior he or she is attempting to modify, and is doing this with consistency, the patient is likely to see therapeutic benefit.

Once patients have identified the EDBs they would like to change, they may still find it difficult to consistently adopt an alternative behavior, particularly in the beginning. As the patient consistently tracks EDBs, he or she is likely to improve his or her ability to engage in the alternative action. However, you may find the motivation enhancement techniques described earlier in this guide to be helpful as well.

Homework

✎ Instruct the patient to continue monitoring progress by completing the OASIS and ODSIS forms and charting the Progress Record.

✎ Have the patient complete the Changing EDBs form in Chapter 10 of the workbook. This form can be used to help patients to modify maladaptive EDBs in response to emotions and situations that arise. This form is also useful in assessing the extent to which patients are applying the concepts in a general fashion, and to aid in coming up with more adaptive action tendencies.

✎ In preparation for emotion exposures, it may be helpful to encourage patients to begin entering situations that may provoke difficult emotions. This could include talking to a friend about a difficult topic, watching a distressing television show or movie, etc. Patients do not yet need to elicit emotions that are personally relevant, per se. It is most important that they begin to practice emotion exposures that are only mildly threatening to get a sense of what it is like to do these activities. Instruct patients to practice being aware of their emotional experience in these situations, including automatic appraisals, avoidance strategies, or EDBs.

Chapter 12 *Module 6: Awareness and Tolerance of Physical Sensations*

(Corresponds to Chapter 11 of the workbook)

Materials Needed

▪ Symptom Induction Test form

▪ Thin straw for symptom induction exercise

▪ Stop watch (or clock with a second hand) for exercises

▪ Any other materials that may be relevant to patient's specific physiological reactivity (e.g., belt for tightening around waist)

▪ Symptom Induction Practice form

Goals

▪ Review homework from previous session

▪ Help the patient identify internal physical sensations associated with his or her emotions

▪ Help the patient gain a greater understanding of the role that internal physical sensations play in determining his or her emotional response

▪ Conduct symptom exercises designed to elicit uncomfortable physical sensations

■ In the same way that thoughts and behaviors can influence emotional experiences, so can physical sensations. Emotions influence how we feel physically, and our physical feelings influence our emotions.

■ Physical sensations can become "signs" that emotions are more intense than they really are and can influence the intensity of the emotional response.

■ Becoming more aware of and comfortable with internal physical feelings can help to put them into perspective and see how they contribute to the overall emotional experience.

■ In order to understand how physical sensations are contributing to uncomfortable emotional experiences, it is crucial to first be able to understand what a physical sensation feels like apart from any interpretations of what it might mean.

Key Concepts

The focus of this chapter is on exposure to physical sensations that can sometimes trigger intense emotions. The exercises described in Chapter 11 of the workbook are designed to assist patients in gaining further awareness of physical sensations that are part of an emotional reaction. In addition, these exercises, and continued exposures focused on physical sensations, will help patients learn to tolerate and think differently about the sensations, and provide an opportunity to break the conditioned association between the sensations and strong emotions such as fear, anxiety, and sadness. In this section, the goals for the patient are to:

■ Increase his or her understanding of the role that physical sensations play in determining emotional responses

■ Identify internal physical sensations associated with his or her emotions

■ Repeatedly engage in exercises designed to help him or her become more aware of physical sensations and increase tolerance of these symptoms

Homework Review

Continue to review the patient's OASIS, ODSIS, and Progress Record forms. Review the patient's completed Changing EDBs form, as well as any additional forms that may have been assigned for further practice. At this point, patients may have been able to identify alternative behaviors to their EDBs, but are unable to implement these new responses. You may wish to work with the patient in examining the specific reasons he or she was unable to move forward with engaging in the new behaviors. In our experience, patients are reluctant to change EDBs because, in doing so, they would be confronting the very emotions they have had difficulty experiencing in the past. Thus, it may be useful to help patients identify and challenge outcome expectancies regarding what they believe will happen if they do not engage in their current EDBs, specifically with regard to their emotions. For instance, a patient may believe that if they do not engage in a particular EDB that the emotion will increase in intensity, or that it will be experienced indefinitely. Addressing these concerns will help the patient to see her EDBs as being non-adaptive, and essentially "clear the path" for new alternative behaviors.

Physical Sensations and the Emotional Response

In the same way that patients learn to recognize thoughts and behaviors as part of the emotional response, it is important for them to have a good understanding of how physical sensations can also contribute to emotions. Emphasize the idea that depending on how patients think about and experience these physical sensations, they can actually contribute to the emotional response. Take the example of a person giving a speech in front of a large audience. If the person begins experiencing an increased heart rate, sweaty palms, lightheadedness, and slight feelings of unreality, and focuses his or her attention on these physical sensations and views them as a threat to his ability to continue with the speech, he or she is likely to experience an intensification of the emotional response (including the physical sensations). In turn, this intense emotional response will cause the person to become even more concerned about the sensations, and so on. If, on the other hand, the person giving the speech sees the sensations as a normal reaction that sometimes occurs in high-pressure situations and does not believe that they significantly interfere with his or her performance, or is accepting of this possible interference, it is more likely that the person will be able to focus his or her attention on the speech and, after a short period of time, the symptoms will diminish on their own.

This initial discussion of the role of physical sensations in the emotional response provides the patient with clear justification for increased exposure to these sensations, and sets the stage for the symptom-induction exercises described below.

Avoidance of Physical Sensations

Avoidance of physical sensations is common in patients suffering from panic disorder. However, in our experience, patients with other anxious and depressive symptoms also exhibit some level of avoidance of physical sensations. More obvious avoidance includes avoiding activities, such as physical exercise, arguments with friends, thrilling movies, or sexual relations, which elicit strong physical sensations. Patients may avoid substances that would naturally produce physical sensations, such as caffeinated beverages, chocolate, energy drinks, and even over-the-counter medications. Avoidance also includes distracting oneself from thoughts about physical sensations. Of course, avoidance precludes relearning, and instead maintains the vigilance for, and acute sensitivity to, such sensations. You will need to work with patients to repeatedly confront physical sensations, so they can learn to tolerate the sensations and associated anxiety, and learn that the sensations are not harmful.

Over the course of a number of such practices, anxiety over the symptoms eventually declines. Having patients systematically face their feared sensations is very different than how they may have experienced these sensations in the past, as those experiences were most likely accompanied by significant fear and avoidance. In this case, patients will work toward embracing rather than avoiding the physical sensations that typify their uncomfortable emotional experiences.

Symptom Induction Exercises

During this part of the treatment, you will work with patients to engage in symptom-induction exercises designed to elicit physical sensations. These exercises will help to increase awareness of physical sensations as part of the emotional response, increase tolerance of these sensations, and reduce patterns of avoidance. A number of specific exercises are described in chapter 11 of the workbook, but you should be creative in trying to develop exercises that will be most relevant, given the patient's presenting symptoms. The Symptom Induction Test Form in chapter 11 of the workbook can be used to assess the patient's response to these exercises. After each exercise, ask the patient to rate the intensity of the physical sensations he or she experienced, the distress associated with the symptoms, and similarity of those symptoms to those that typically occur as part of an emotional response. Each of these items is rated on a 0–8 point scale, with 0 being the least intense, distressing, and/or not at all similar and 8 being extremely intense, distressing, and/or most similar. Based on the results of this assessment, several exercises can be selected for additional practice in-session, or given to the patient as homework. Choose exercises that are at least moderately distressing to the patient and are most similar to the symptoms that occur naturally during an emotional response.

The symptom induction exercises are to be performed in a way that elicits sensations as strongly as possible. Although patients may only be able to engage in the exercises for a short period of time initially, the length of exposure gradually can be extended. However, it is important that the sensations are fully induced, and that the patient continues with exposure beyond the point that the sensations are initially experienced. Terminating the exercises on first noticing the sensations will reinforce fear of the symptoms. The awareness skills developed earlier in treatment should also be brought to bear during the exercises. Instruct patients to focus on the sensations while conducting the exercises, not to distract from them. If patients notice certain thoughts occurring during the exercises, they should not engage in cognitive reappraisal at this point, but rather should simply notice them as part of the experience. All forms of avoidance (e.g., distraction, minimal symptom induction, the presence of safety signals) should be prevented in order for patients to obtain the most benefits from the exposures.

Therapist Note:

■ *Before conducting the symptom induction exercises, it is important to fully assess for any medical conditions that would render these exercises harmful for the patient. It is also important to differentiate psychological distress from true potential for harm. For example, a patient diagnosed with panic disorder who fears having a heart attack while running in place (in the absence of any physical heart condition), is different from a patient who could be put at risk for cardiac arrest due to a documented medical condition.* ■

Repeated Exposures

After identifying exercises that elicit physical sensations most similar to the patient's naturally occurring symptoms, ask the patient to engage in the exercises repeatedly, either in-session or as homework. The duration of exposure to sensations gradually can be lengthened so that the intensity of sensations either remains the same or increases. The level of distress, however, eventually decreases as the patient becomes better able to endure the sensations. The same induction exercise is conducted repeatedly, with the patient only waiting long enough in between "trials" for the symptoms to mostly subside. The exercise is then repeated until the patient's distress reaches a 2 or less. Patients should continue with the same exercise again the next day, or soon thereafter. On subsequent trials, the level of distress is likely to be less than where it started previously, but may be slightly higher than it was at the end of the last exercise. This continued exposure helps facilitate learning and may prevent any distress about these sensations from returning long term.

Case Vignettes

Case Vignette #1

In the following case vignette, the therapist is explaining why hyperventilation can cause physical sensations.

P: Why does hyperventilating cause all those physical sensations I feel?

T: That's a good question. Without going into too much detail, hyperventilation essentially leads to low levels of carbon dioxide in the blood. This causes many of the symptoms you may feel if you hyperventilate. For instance, low carbon dioxide levels cause the brain's blood vessels to constrict, resulting in a slight reduction of blood flow to the brain, which results in feelings of lightheadedness. Breathing slowly, or just allowing your body to regulate itself, will bring the balance of oxygen and carbon dioxide back to normal and the physical symptoms will naturally diminish.

Case Vignette #2

In the following case vignette, the therapist is explaining why the hyperventilation exercise is not likely to cause fainting.

P: Won't I faint if I do the hyperventilation exercise?

T: The short answer is no. At least, it would be highly unlikely, unless you're especially prone to fainting. When people faint, it's usually due to a sudden drop in blood pressure or heart rate. This is not what happens during hyperventilation. It's possible to pass out from hyperventilating, but that typically occurs only when people hyperventilate for long periods of time or when they immediately hold their breath afterwards. Our exercise is not really long enough to cause this to happen. However, it is likely to produce some physical sensations that may be slightly uncomfortable, including lightheadedness, increased heart rate, and tingling in your hands and face. Those are normal sensations and do not necessarily mean that you're going to faint.

Case Vignette #3

In the following case vignette, the therapist provides a rationale for why the patient should practice interoceptive exercises even if they don't feel particularly afraid of any physical sensations.

P: I don't think I'm really afraid of any physical sensations. Do you think we should still go through the exercises?

T: Yes I do. Even if you're not afraid of physical sensations, the exercises will give you a chance to really focus on the sensations and build your awareness of this component of the emotional response. Essentially, you can practice awareness of the physical changes that happen in your body. Then, when you experience a strong emotional reaction, you'll be better able to notice the physical reaction that occurs as part of the emotional response.

Case Vignette #4

In the following case vignette, the therapist provides the patient with guidelines for deciding when to stop practicing the hyperventilation exercises.

P: Hyperventilating makes me feel lightheaded and tingly no matter how many times I do it. When should I stop doing it?

T: Do you feel distressed when you become lightheaded or tingly?

P: Not anymore, I was originally....it really bothered me...but now it's just uncomfortable. I don't like it too much, but it doesn't make me anxious or anything.

T: If you are no longer distressed by the sensations, there is no need to continue with the exercise. Remember, the exercises are not designed to eliminate the sensations but to lessen your distress about the sensations. You might want to come back to it from time to time, just to practice, but otherwise I think you can move on to another exercise.

Some patients do not report much distress during the symptom induction exercises. There are a number of reasons why this might occur. Depending on the presenting symptoms, some patients may not experience much distress when completing these exercises, while other patients may find them more difficult. Also, some patients may need to engage in exercises that are different than those listed in the workbook. You should work collaboratively with the patient to identify any avoidance of physical sensations, and then use this information to construct an exercise that is more likely to elicit distress. You should also be aware that some patients discontinue the exercises before they fully experience physical sensations. They may terminate the exercises as soon as the sensations are felt, or may not perform the exercises with the intensity needed to fully produce physical sensations. Be sure to address such avoidance and help patients modify their anxious beliefs regarding this situation. Even when patients don't report much distress when completing the exercises, they should still be asked to conduct them repeatedly to help facilitate greater awareness of the physical sensations when they occur in other contexts.

Occasionally, patients report difficulty completing the symptom exercises at home. Often, this is because the perceived safety of the therapist, or the therapeutic environment, is no longer present. Patients become concerned that if they experience strong physical sensations they will not recover as easily from the experience, or that it may lead to more intense emotions. Help patients identify the perceived consequences and work with them to put things back into perspective (i.e., *"What's the worst than can happen?"*). A graduated approach can also be used. Patients could begin the exercises in the presence of a friend or family member or even in the therapist's office with the therapist out of the room. Next, the patient would practice alone.

Sometimes patients only experience distress about the sensations when they are in certain situations, but not others. Usually this is due to how the patient is thinking about the sensations within that particular context. For instance, having feelings of lightheadedness may be perceived as being much more dangerous if experienced while driving than in some other situation. Examine the kind of thoughts that make the symptoms appear more dangerous in those situations. Remind the patient that, in reality, the symptoms are no more harmful in that situation than they are in other situations, including the therapist's office.

Homework

 Instruct the patient to continue monitoring progress by completing the OASIS and ODSIS forms, and charting the Progress Record.

Instruct the patient to repeatedly engage in physical sensation exposures using the Symptom Induction Practice Form in Chapter 11 of the workbook. This form can be used to help patients conduct symptom induction exercises at home. Assign three brief physical sensation exposure exercises, to be agreed upon in session.

Chapter 13 *Module 7: Interoceptive and Situational Emotion Exposures*

(Corresponds to Chapter 12 of the workbook)

Materials Needed

- Emotion induction exercise materials (patient-specific)

- Emotional and Situational Avoidance Hierarchy

- Record of Emotion Exposure Practice

Goals

- Review homework from previous session

- Help the patient to understand the purpose of emotion exposures

- Work with the patient to develop an emotional and situational avoidance hierarchy

- Design effective emotion exposure exercises

- Assist patients in confronting strong emotions through emotion exposure exercises

Summary of Information in Chapter 12 of UP Workbook

- In order to learn new ways of responding to emotionally intense situations, it is necessary to conduct exercises to intentionally bring on these types of emotional experiences.

- *Emotion exposures* involve gradually confronting internal and external stimuli that may produce strong or intense emotional reactions.

- Emotion exposures can occur in the context of internal situations, such as thoughts, memories, or even physical sensations. Emotion exposures can also occur in external situations that are likely to bring on intense emotional reactions and may be currently avoided.

- Emotion exposures should be conducted without any avoidance, and each exposure should be used as an opportunity to change maladaptive EDBs.

Key Concepts

The primary focus of this chapter is emotion exposures. Emotion exposures are exercises designed specifically to provoke strong emotional responses. Following a brief introduction to the concept of emotion exposures, and rationale for engaging in these exercises, you will assist patients in gradually confronting internal and external stimuli that produce intense emotional reactions and help them modify their responses to those emotions. You will help patients incorporate the skills learned in therapy (e.g., present-focused awareness, nonjudgment, cognitive reappraisal) into their exposure practice, and address any emotional avoidance that impedes treatment progress. In this section, the goals for the patient are to:

- Gain an understanding of the purpose of emotion exposures.

- Learn to develop a fear and avoidance hierarchy, and learn how to design effective emotion exposure exercises.

- Repeatedly practice confronting strong emotions through emotion exposure exercises.

Homework Review

Following a review of the patient's OASIS, ODSIS, and Progress Record forms, as well as any additional forms that may have been assigned for further practice, review the patient's Symptom Induction Practice form. Was the patient able to practice the symptom induction exercises that were assigned? As noted in the previous chapter, there are a number of reasons why patients might have difficulty completing these exercises at home. Work with the patient on identifying specific reasons the exercises were not completed and then collaboratively develop a plan for addressing these difficulties. You can also work with the patient on completing the exercises in-session as emotion exposures. Review additional homework forms that were assigned from previous chapters. If the patient is having difficulty completing these forms, you may want to review key concepts from past sessions.

Emotion Exposures

The remainder of treatment focuses on exposure to internal and external stimuli that may produce strong or intense emotional reactions. We refer to these exposures as *emotion exposures* because the primary focus of the exposure is not the specific situation, image, or activity, but rather the emotion itself. This part of treatment will likely be the most difficult for patients, but is an opportunity for them to put the skills they have learned into practice (such as nonjudgmental present-focused awareness, identifying automatic appraisals, and countering emotional avoidance and EDBs), so that once treatment is finished they will be confident in their ability to handle future emotional experiences as they unfold. It is very important that patients commit to making time and effort during this last part of treatment, because this is the chance for real changes to occur.

Therapist Note:

The goal of the emotion exposures is not immediate reduction in the emotional response. Rather, the goal is for patients to learn something new as a result of the experience. Consistent with a focus on emotions and emotion regulation, conceptually all exposures are directed towards patients experiencing their emotions fully (which means reducing patterns of avoidance) and implementing new responses. Tolerance of emotions is a critical learning goal of emotion exposures.

With regard to changing how patients experience and respond to their emotions, emotion exposures are important for the following reasons:

1. Interpretations and appraisals about the dangerousness of situations (whether they are internal or external in nature) begin to change and newer, more adaptive interpretations and appraisals begin to emerge.

2. Avoidance, and subsequent impairment, is reversed.

3. EDBs can be recognized and modified.

Exposure serves to develop a new set of nonfearful associations between the stimulus (e.g., giving a presentation), response (e.g., feeling light-headed), and meaning (e.g., "I'm not making any sense...I'm failing"). The new association (e.g., feeling lightheaded during a presentation does not mean that I'm failing) gradually becomes more salient over time and old, fearful associations are forgotten.

Introduction to In-Session Emotion Exposures

In-session emotion exposures help patients learn how to conduct emotion exposures, while processing emotions immediately with the therapist. While not always feasible, in-session exposures should be conducted whenever possible. When you conduct an exposure with the patient during the treatment session, you are in a good position to give corrective feedback and clear instruction, provide participant modeling, and facilitate the patient's tolerance of emotions during the exercise.

The particular exposure tasks will vary from patient to patient. The Emotional and Situational Avoidance Hierarchy form in Chapter 12 of the workbook can be used to get an idea of the types of situations that trigger uncomfortable emotions for patients, and the situations that are most often avoided. Several types of emotion exposure exercises are detailed in the workbook. These include situationally based, imaginal, and interoceptive emotion exposures. All of these exercises can be used to assist patients in practicing skills they have learned during the course of treatment. With any of the in-session exposures, make sure to leave at least 15 minutes of time in-session to process the exposure with the patient.

Therapist Note:

■ *When designing exposures, it is important to consider that uncomfortable or aversive emotions can be negative or positive in valence. For example, a patient struggling with recurrent worry and tension may find it difficult to fully engage in a pleasurable activity and "leave their worries behind." The experience of positive emotions may evoke anxiety about "being off guard." Similarly, a patient struggling with obsessive doubts may find it difficult to enjoy dinner out with friends. Allowing themselves to be fully present in the moment without retreating into engagement with intrusive thoughts may be particularly anxiety provoking. Therefore, it may be important to design emotion exposures around both negative and positive emotional experiences.* ■

Conducting In-Session Emotion Exposures

Once the specific emotion exposure task has been identified, spend time with the patient preparing for the exposure by engaging in some or all of the following steps before attempting a task:

1. Agree upon a specific task that will be completed (usually drawn from the Emotional and Situational Avoidance Hierarchy).

2. Discuss anxious or negative thoughts occurring prior to initiating the task, or those that are expected to occur during the task, and consider more rational alternatives.

3. Remind the patient of the importance of using present-focused awareness of his or her emotions during the exposure.

4. Identify avoidance behaviors that are likely to interfere with the exposure, and EDBs that will be modified.

You should structure the task in a way that best permits new learning to occur. This involves some level of clarification of what it is that the patient is most worried about happening, so that the exposure can then be directed towards challenging those negative outcome expectancies. If what the patient is most concerned about is the emotional response itself, then the corrective learning is about the patient's ability to tolerate sustained levels of a negative emotion. With all emotion exposures, it is extremely important for the therapist to "catch" any moments where patients are avoiding their emotions, either by changing the topic, "breaking" the role of the exposure, fidgeting, etc. As soon as you notice these responses, make the patients aware that they are avoiding the full emotional experience and redirect their attention back to the emotion.

During in-session exercises, it is important to be directive and confident and to encourage patients to continue the exposure despite experiencing intense and uncomfortable emotions. Be careful not to reinforce the patient's perceived inability to tolerate negative emotions, and don't collude with the patient in engaging in patterns of avoidance, as noted earlier. It is important that you do not suggest to the patient that a particular situation may be too difficult or too distressing, or over-empathize with the patient's distress during the exposures. Therefore, early on it may be best to choose activities toward the middle of the patient's hierarchy so that the likelihood of success is high. This will allow patients to gain a sense of mastery over an aversive experience, while simultaneously becoming more tolerant of their emotions. Over time, you will help the patient gradually and systematically work up the hierarchy.

After the exposure takes place, spend at least 15 minutes processing it. You may wish to use the Three-Component Model of Emotions form to help patients explore their emotional experience during the in-session exposures. Ask about patients' emotions before the exposure, and what thoughts and physical sensations came up during the task. Also, it is important to note any avoidance behaviors and EDBs. Identifying ways to increase the level of difficulty of the exposures, and discussing ways to make the exposures more effective, can also be very helpful. Outline the accomplishments the patient made and ways that he or she could improve the emotion exposures. The patient should always receive positive reinforcement for at least attempting an exposure.

Moving Emotion Exposures into the Real World

A crucial factor in the success of treatment lies in the patient's continued practice of emotion exposures outside of session (*in vivo* exposures). Moving exposures into the real world is important for several reasons. First, practicing in vivo emotion exposures allows patients to directly apply the skills they have learned in treatment to the context of their daily lives. Second, practicing in vivo exposures allows patients to develop a sense of autonomy or agency in their own treatment, facilitating the transition away from the therapist and toward independence. Finally, the actual time spent in therapy represents approximately 1% of the patient's waking hours; therefore, in order to truly learn skills presented in therapy, it is essential that the patient continues to practice skills outside of session.

The therapist and patient should work together to design emotion exposures that can be practiced outside of the therapy session. Again, the Emotional and Situational Avoidance Hierarchy in Chapter 12 of the workbook can be used to identify possible emotion exposures. For example, a patient struggling with panic symptoms may take a crowded subway to work. A patient struggling with social phobia may purposely engage in a conversation with an unfamiliar coworker. Or, a person with intrusive and distressing thoughts may write down their most feared thoughts and read them aloud daily.

Using the Record of Emotion Exposure Practice form in Chapter 12 of the workbook, patients should be encouraged to record their experiences with completing emotion exposures. Spend time processing exposures practiced over the week at the start of the following session, paying particular attention to any patterns of emotional avoidance or obstacles that may have stood in the way of successful completion of exposures. As noted, a patient should always receive positive reinforcement for any attempt at an exposure, and you and the patient should work together toward making exposures optimally effective, and continually increasing their difficulty.

Case Vignettes

Case Vignette #1

In the following case vignette, the therapist clarifies the intended purpose of emotion exposures and provides guidance on how to most effectively complete these tasks.

P: I conducted the emotion exposure we had discussed. I rode the subway for the entire time I was supposed to, but my fear never became less. I was terrified.

T: That's great!

P: How's that great!? I felt awful. I didn't like being scared. I kept thinking it was going to get better but it never did.

T: The point of the emotion exposures is not to be able to do them without any fear. It's really about how you experience and respond to your fear that's most important. We purposely selected that situation because we knew it would scare you. We wanted you to learn a couple of things. First, as we discussed, it was important for you to expose yourself to this particular situation for you to see that what you thought was going to happen didn't actually happen. In fact, it turned out much better than you thought it would. Second, we wanted you to work toward developing a greater tolerance of your emotions, in this case a feeling of fear. The important point here is that despite feeling afraid, you stayed the entire time.

P: Do you think it will be better next time? I mean, will I eventually be less afraid?

T: It's likely that by continuing to ride the subway, the fear will gradually begin to decrease. But that depends on whether you attempt to avoid your emotions in that situation, or do something to make the situation less frightening.

P: Why does that matter again?

T: Well as we've discussed, engaging in avoidance prevents you from really learning that the situation is not dangerous. In this case, you were afraid that your fear might become so intense that you would lose control of yourself or that you might go crazy.

P: Definitely. So you're saying that if I just allow my fear to be there, and don't do anything to avoid it, that eventually it will diminish?

T: Again, it sort of depends on you. In general, I would suggest that you focus more on reducing patterns of avoidance and changing EDBs, rather than worrying so much about what happens to your fear. Now it's important to be aware of the emotional experience, and maybe you can even do a quick three-point check to notice your thoughts, feelings, and behaviors as the emotion unfolds. But then it's just about riding the wave. Just allow the emotion to be there and then notice what happens as a result. Are you losing your mind? Are you doing anything uncontrollable? If you don't do anything to avoid or escape, then you'll be in the best position to learn that your fear is not dangerous in this situation, and chances are the emotion will eventually decrease.

Case Vignette #2

In the following case vignette, the therapist helps the patient identify the anxious cognitions they experienced when attempting an emotion exposure.

P: I stayed at the meeting for a little while, but eventually I had to get out of there.

T: And why was that?

P: Well, I started feeling really upset. My vision got blurry and I was having trouble focusing on what my boss was saying.

T: So, then what happened?

P: Well I excused myself from the meeting and went outside to get some air. I really tried to stay but the feelings got so intense. I knew that if I just stayed a little longer, something bad might happen.

T: Why did you feel the need to protect yourself against those feelings? What are your thoughts about what could have happened if you stayed?

P: I was just concerned that I might say something stupid because I couldn't really focus properly...on account of the feelings I was having.

T: It looks like maybe we should take some time to look a little more closely at these thoughts you have about your emotions.

Case Vignette #3

In the following case vignette, the therapist assists the patient in developing strategies for modifying their EDBs during an emotion exposure.

P: I keep leaving the situation too early, right when my emotion hits the peak. What do you think I should do to keep myself in it?

T: It's tough sometimes to go against our EDBs, especially when those behaviors have been reinforced so much in the past. I mean, at this point, you know that escaping from that situation will make you feel relieved. So it's hard not to do that. But I think there are a couple of things you might do here. You could try choosing a situation that's a little further down on your hierarchy. Maybe choose something that's likely to be a little less frightening, but that you feel you'll really be able to stay in. Also, you could purposely put yourself in a situation where escape is difficult, or ask a friend or family member to assist you with staying in the situation when you're feeling frightened. How does that sound?

P: That sounds pretty good. It helps when I have something to remind me to come back to the three components we talked about in the past. Maybe I'll just make out a little note card that I can fill in while I'm completing the exposure.

T: I like that idea. Also, remember that if you escape from a situation prematurely, you can always think about the situation a little when the emotions aren't as high and then try to go back into the situation as soon as possible.

Managing Problems

Sometimes, when patients are not fully "on board" with the rationale for conducting emotion exposures they might choose "easy" exposures, or exposures that are not likely to provoke significant symptoms. In these cases, continuing to go through the exercises will not be helpful. If the patient is unwilling to face uncomfortable emotions, then the time should be spent revisiting prior treatment concepts to assist the patient in eventually engaging in the emotion exposures. You may also find the motivation enhancement techniques described in chapter 5 useful.

As illustrated in Case Vignette #3, occasionally, patients may escape from a situation if their emotions become too strong during emotion exposures. If escapes happen, it should not be regarded as a failure. Rather, this can be presented as an opportunity for the patient to learn from it. Escape is a clear EDB that typically occurs in response to a fear reaction, and is usually based on the prediction that continued endurance will result in some kind of negative outcome. For example, it is not uncommon for patients to believe that if they stay in the situation their anxiety or fear will become so intense that the emotion will become out of control and they will be unable to function. You should help the patient evaluate this prediction in terms of the thinking traps of jumping to conclusions and catastrophizing. From there, the patient should be encouraged to reenter the situation as soon as possible.

Patients can sometimes be discouraged by the pace at which exposures occur. Also, it can be frustrating to patients when they notice a decrease in their emotion to a situation over time, only to then reexperience strong emotions in the same situation at a later point. In these cases, it can be important to remind the patient that learning is rarely linear and that, just like any other time of learning, some forgetting occurs over time. Also, learning tends to be fairly context-dependent, so changing things up even a little bit can sometimes cause a return of the symptoms that they thought had been completely diminished. The recurrence of their emotional response to these situations should not be taken as a failure, or an indication that exposures do not work. Rather, it should be viewed as another opportunity to learn that they can tolerate their emotions, and that the situation is not dangerous. These recurrences provide excellent learning opportunities and can actually help them generalize what they learned in one situation to other, similar situations as well. Again, the goal of treatment is for patients to be less distressed by their emotions (and the situations that provoke them) and to respond more adaptively—the goal is not to prevent them from happening.

Homework

✎ Instruct the patient to continue monitoring progress by completing the OASIS and ODSIS forms and charting the Progress Record.

✎ Have the patient practice emotion exposures at least three times over the next week, and record practice on the Record of Emotion Exposure Practice form in the workbook. As treatment progresses, exposures should increase in difficulty and the patient should be encouraged to take more responsibility for designing exposures.

Chapter 14 *Medications for Anxiety, Depression, and Related Emotional Disorders*

(Corresponds to Chapter 13 of the workbook)

Therapist Note:

■ *This chapter provides information for the therapist, and does not correspond to a particular therapy session. Therefore, there are no goals or materials needed. There are no homework assignments either. Discontinuation of medication is usually addressed toward the end of therapy when patients are beginning to feel better and more confident in their ability to manage their symptoms without medicine.* ■

Summary of Information in Chapter 13 of UP Workbook

■ Reasons for medication use.

■ Description of most commonly used medications.

■ Information on how medications can be discontinued.

Introduction to Medication Issues

There is tremendous variability in the extent to which individuals use medication, psychological treatment (such as this program), or some combination of the two. We don't really talk about medication as a more or less effective form of treatment in general, but as more or less appropriate depending on the situation. Under ordinary circumstances, medications are likely to begin to exert beneficial effects in a shorter period of time than a psychological treatment program, such as this program. This is especially true of the benzodiazepines, which can be effective almost immediately to within a matter of a few days. Antidepressant medication such as selective serotonin reuptake inhibitors (SSRIs) and serotonin-norepinephrine reuptake inhibitors (SNRIs), widely regarded as the first-choice medication treatments for most anxiety and mood disorders, take longer to be metabolized into the blood stream and begin to exert their effects, often as long as 3 to 6 weeks. On the other hand, medications can sometimes lose some of their effectiveness when taken continuously over an extended period. In addition, there may be a greater risk of relapse when the medication is discontinued. This program may be beneficial for individuals who have achieved some relief from medication, or who are hoping to prevent long-term use of such medications.

It is important to describe how medications can interact with, and sometimes even interfere with, treatment procedures. For a number of disorders, particularly panic disorder, combination medication and cognitive-behavioral treatments have been shown to have poorer treatment outcomes over the long term than individual cognitive-behavioral treatments. Although this does not appear to be the case with depression, where combination medication and cognitive behavioral treatment appear to be somewhat more effective than either treatment alone, at least in the short term. Beyond overall treatment outcome, it is important to note that fast-acting medications, such as benzodiazepines, may interfere with exposures by either preventing levels of emotion from reaching peak intensity, or functioning as safety signals. In both cases, the use of fast-acting medications may prevent the new learning that naturally occurs during exposures.

A number of patients who come into treatment mention getting off of their medications as one of their treatment goals. This is common, and the application of the techniques described in this program is appropriate and can be helpful for patients. Withdrawal or reduction in medication use must be undertaken only under the direct supervision of a physician. However, the increase in anxious or depressed mood that often occurs following gradual withdrawal and discontinuation of medications can be targeted with the techniques outlined in this protocol. If withdrawal from medications is particularly difficult (as might often be the case when withdrawing from benzodiazepines), then the program described in the book *Stopping Anxiety Medication, Therapist Guide, 2nd Edition* (Otto & Pollack, 2009) from the Treatments *ThatWork*™ series might be helpful.

Case Vignettes

The following vignettes illustrate different aspects of discussing medications with patients.

Case Vignette #1

P: I thought that the medication was necessary to correct my chemical imbalance.

T: That is actually a commonly held belief. However, to date, there is no clear evidence of a specific chemical imbalance that is a primary cause of anxiety or depression. The question of how the medications work isn't well understood, except that they do seem to reduce the intensity of the symptoms experienced. Regardless of how the medications work, it is still important to learn that you can cope with emotions, even if you do experience more intense symptoms.

Case Vignette #2

P: Can I take my medication with me during (or before I do) the exposure?

T: What makes you think you need to take your medication with you during the exposure?

P: I don't think I'll need them. I mean, I haven't taken them in months, but I want to have them in case my emotions get too intense.

T: Have you had any intense emotions over the past few months?

P: Yes, many times. Especially during some of the recent exposures we've been doing.

T: Ok, so in that last exposure, did you take your medication?

P: No, I didn't have it with me.

T: What happened to your emotions?

P: Well, they got really intense, but I guess they came back down on their own.

T: So if your emotions came back down on their own, what role do you think taking your medication into this exposure might play?

P: I guess they could actually be a safety signal and might prevent me from fully engaging in the exposure, and may even prevent my emotions from coming down as quickly as they naturally would on their own.

Case Vignette #3

P: I'm afraid that my emotions are going to become even more severe when I withdraw from the medication, and I'll be right back where I started.

T: Specifically, what do you mean when you say that your emotions would become more severe?

P: You know, out of control like they were before I started this treatment.

T: Ok. How would you respond to those emotions now?

P: Well, I suppose I would try to apply the skills we've learned in treatment.

T: Great! What would that look like, specifically?

P: First I would do a three-point check and identify the thoughts, feelings, and behaviors of my emotional response. Next, I would explore the context of my emotional response by looking at the ARC of my response. Then I would use my anchoring in the present skills to bring myself to the here and now, so that I could more objectively reappraise the situation.

T: So it sounds like you've learned quite a bit about your emotions and how to respond to them effectively.

P: I guess I have.

T: Given how much you've learned, and that you've already changed how you experience and respond to your emotions once, how do you think you would respond even if your emotions did become more frequent and intense?

P: Well, I guess I'd work through the treatment procedures again. If I've done it once, it must be easier the second time.

Managing Problems

As illustrated in Case Vignette #1, patients often have preconceived notions about the nature of emotional disorders and the need for medications to correct chemical imbalances in the brain. These beliefs can increase a patient's anxiety or apprehension about withdrawing from medication. Brief psychoeducation about the research on the nature of emotional disorders can be helpful in allowing patients to make a more informed decision about continuing or withdrawing from medication.

Patients can come to rely on their medication as a safety signal. This most often occurs with benzodiazepines, but can also occur with other medications as well. As shown in Case Vignette #2, it is important for the therapist to address this directly in treatment, as using benzodiazepines prior to the exposure, or even just taking them into the exposure without using them, can reduce the effectiveness of the exposure.

Another common fear described by patients is that their emotions or symptoms will become more severe and intense once they discontinue medication, and that they will be right back where they started before treatment. As illustrated in Case Vignette #3, it is helpful to point out to patients how much they have learned and how far they have come already. Even if they do have a recurrence of their symptoms, they have developed a new way of responding to them that they did not previously have. Thus, they will never really be right back where they started.

Chapter 15 *Module 8: Accomplishments, Maintenance, and Relapse Prevention*

(Corresponds to Chapter 14 of the workbook)

Materials Needed

- Practice Plan
- Long-Term Goals form

Goals

- Review homework from previous session
- Review skills for coping with emotions
- Review treatment progress
- Identify and troubleshoot common/potential triggers
- Promote skill generalization and set goals for continued progress

Summary of Information in Chapter 14 of UP Workbook

- Practicing treatment skills will help maintain treatment gains and promote continued progress. This includes maintaining awareness of emotions, engaging in cognitive reappraisal, reducing emotion avoidance, and practicing emotion exposures and modifying EDBs.

- Fluctuation in symptoms is natural and normal, and does not necessarily mean that relapse has occurred.

- Practice plans can be used to promote continued practice of treatment skills following the end of the treatment program.

- Ongoing evaluation is important for noticing changes in symptoms that may need to be addressed, and to prevent maladaptive cycles of emotions from developing.

Key Concepts

The purpose of this chapter is evaluating the patient's progress and planning for the future. You will also reinforce the skills learned in treatment, review key treatment concepts, and help patients develop strategies for preventing "relapse." Additionally, this chapter is used to address symptom recurrence and how patients can maintain treatment gains in the long term.

In this section, the goals for the patient are to:

- Review key treatment concepts and skills for coping with emotions.

- Evaluate treatment progress and areas for improvement.

- Set short-term and long-term goals for maintaining treatment gains and for continued progress.

Homework Review

Review the patient's continued progress with completing homework assignments. You may find it useful to compare changes on more recent assignments with homework completed earlier in treatment, to identify improvement that has occurred over the course of the program. Further, assessing the patient's ability to complete homework assignments during treatment is important for discussing short-term and long-term goals for maintaining treatment gains and for continued progress.

Review of Treatment Skills

This chapter begins with a review of treatment skills. In Chapter 14 of the workbook, patients are provided with several "steps" they can take to respond adaptively to uncomfortable emotions. Review these steps with the patient by presenting the patient with a scenario that is consistent with his or her presenting symptoms, and then asking the patient how they would go about responding adaptively to the emotions he or she is likely to experience. Using an example that is personally relevant will help the patient to more easily appreciate his or her ability to handle these situations now and in the future, thus promoting a greater sense of efficacy as the patient terminates treatment

Evaluating Progress

Help the patient evaluate his or her progress in treatment to this point. Instead of simply focusing on how the patient feels now, in general, compared to how the patient remembers feeling at the beginning of treatment, use data from the monitoring records that were completed throughout the course of treatment. We typically enter each patient's weekly ratings from the OASIS and ODSIS into a data spreadsheet and make graphs summarizing this information. This provides patients with a visual record of their progress. This can also be used to generate discussion about their progress in treatment, and to identify areas for improvement.

It is important for patients to think about change and improvement as a continuing process, consistent with learning any new set of responses and skills. Continued improvement following treatment is very typical, as patients have additional opportunity to practice and apply the skills they have learned.

You can also assist patients in understanding reasons for a lack of progress, when this occurs. Reasons might include initial error in diagnosis, lack of understanding of the treatment principles, the need for more time to practice the therapeutic strategies, unrealistic goals, and lack of motivation for practice. Lack of progress is not presented as a hopeless outcome. Instead, these possible reasons are explored with the patient to determine the best course of action that can be taken next, in order for the patient to progress. In this way, the end of treatment can actually be thought of and presented as an opportunity to engage in a "new phase" of treatment, in which the patient can work toward overcoming prior obstacles and achieve greater gains.

Anticipating Future Difficulties

All patients will experience intense or uncomfortable emotions in the future, which often occur in response to life stressors. However, everyone experiences fluctuations in their emotional life—the ups and downs of everyday existence. Sometimes strong emotions can occur that may not appear to directly correlate with any overt stressors. This can be quite distressing to patients, and such experiences can serve as strong triggers for relapse. Throughout the course of treatment, patients have been developing a more detached, less judgmental stance toward their emotional experiences. As treatment is concluded and the focus turns to promoting skill generalization, it is essential to help patients to bring this same nonjudgmental stance to bear on the inevitable ups and downs they will experience once treatment is terminated.

Addressing patient expectations regarding the recurrence of symptoms is an effective strategy for preempting the possibility that symptom recurrence might spiral into full-blown syndrome relapse. Help patients understand that fluctuation of symptoms is natural and normal, and does not mean they have relapsed. If the patient experiences a recurrence of symptoms, including anxiety, depression, and avoidance of internal and external stimuli, this is not a sign that underlying problems are resurfacing to uncontrollable levels, or that treatment did not work. Instead, it means that there is a temporary reappearance of old habits that can be addressed in the same ways learned through the workbook.

Continuing Practice

In an effort to promote continuing progress following the end of treatment, you may wish to work with the patient to identify areas for further practice. Using the Practice Plan form in Chapter 14 of the workbook, work with the patient to generate a list of specific things he or she would like to practice in the coming weeks.

We also recommend that patients set aside time each week to review progress and develop or revise a plan for moving forward. This gives them an opportunity to take stock in what they have accomplished, which can be very motivating. Also, they are in a good position to notice any recurrence of their symptoms, and to prevent maladaptive patterns of emotional responding from developing. This can be especially helpful immediately after the end of treatment, usually for several weeks, but could be continued indefinitely or for as long as the patient finds it useful.

Establishing Long-Term Goals

Now that treatment is ending, and as patients experience improvement in their functioning, they may begin planning for things they were previously unable to do because of their symptoms. Using the Long-Term Goals form in Chapter 14 of the workbook, work with the patient to set long-term Goals and the steps needed to achieve those goals.

Ending Treatment

Patients frequently express concern about ending treatment. It is important to emphasize that patients now have the knowledge and necessary skills to manage and more effectively respond to their emotions.

Case Vignettes

In each of the following vignettes, the patient is coming to terms with the end of treatment.

Case Vignette #1

P: I feel like I've made some real progress, but I'm worried about stopping treatment. I guess I'm a little scared that if my symptoms come back,

I won't remember what we talked about, or how to apply the skills I've learned.

T: I agree that you've made some real progress in treatment, and I can understand why you might be concerned. But, remember, over the course of treatment, you've been developing important skills for responding more adaptively to your emotions. I would say that you now have a good understanding of these skills, and if you continue to practice what you've learned, I imagine you'll become even better at applying these skills over time. I guess it's sort of like any class you may have taken. You don't simply forget everything you've learned just because the class is over. But in order to really retain that information, you may need to continue practicing it, or at least revisit it from time to time.

Case Vignette #2

P: We're at our last session but I still feel anxious and sad sometimes. I get worried that things might get worse after treatment is over. I wish I was cured.

T: I can understand your concern. Ending treatment can be difficult. But remember, our work was never about eliminating your emotions. Feeling anxious and sad sometimes is perfectly normal, as these emotions can be very adaptive under certain conditions. So I wouldn't equate being "cured" with not experiencing these emotions. In fact, thinking this way can get you into some real trouble. Just take one situation at a time, and come back to the skills you've learned. As you come back to these skills and continue to practice them, they'll become second nature. Over time, I think it will be even easier for you to experience your emotions and respond to them in adaptive ways.

Case Vignette #3

P: I know I need to keep doing emotion exposures, but I'm afraid that once I stop coming in for treatment I won't be able to make any additional progress. I don't have anyone to help me review my progress or give me feedback on how to do things differently.

T: Do you mean you aren't sure how to set up the exposures properly on your own?

P: No, I definitely know how to set them up, and I've been pretty good about doing them over the past few weeks. I'm just not sure I have the discipline to make myself practice. Coming in here each week and talking with you has been very motivating for me.

T: I can see how coming in each week may have provided some structure and helped you stay on task with completing the exposures. But I wonder if there might be some other ways to stay motivated. For instance, we talked about setting up your own weekly sessions to review your progress and develop a plan for completing exposures. You can even keep the same time you've been coming to treatment. What other things could you try?

P: Well I guess I could ask my husband to help me stay motivated, as well. Maybe I could even sit down with him and go over the progress I make each week. He's very supportive and I'm sure he would be willing to help out.

T: I think that's a good idea. Also, some people find it useful to give themselves little rewards for completing their practices. You can do this for a little while, and then eventually the benefits from practicing become motivation enough to keep going.

P: I really like that idea! It's always good to get rewards.

Managing Problems

Patients can sometimes feel discouraged at the end of treatment, and sometimes minimize the improvements they have made. As previously noted, using data from the weekly tracking forms can help patients to more accurately evaluate their levels of change. If patients discount the improvements they have made in favor of dwelling on the negative, you may find it helpful to point out these specific negative appraisals and then help them to consider the situation in other ways. For instance, you might emphasize that even though there is still room for improvement, the patient has worked hard to get to this point and has made considerable progress in addressing his or her symptoms. It may also be helpful for patients to think about treatment as more of an ongoing process that occurs even after the formal program has ended, as opposed to something which has a definitive endpoint. In this way, the inability to achieve complete remission of symptoms by the end of treatment is not viewed as a failure, nor is it an indication that additional improvements cannot be made.

Sometimes, major life crises occur toward the end of treatment. Depending on how the patient responds to the situation, he or she may actually regress a bit and feel as though he or she is back at "square one." If this happens, acknowledge the setback but remind the patient that this does not mean that all progress has been lost. Reviewing records kept throughout treatment can be encouraging. By reviewing these records together, you can help the patient recognize that he or she has made progress before, and realize that he or she can certainly do it again.

As illustrated in Case Vignettes #1 and #3, some patients will feel they are not yet ready to end treatment, or express uncertainty about their ability to continue to progress or to maintain what they have achieved once treatment ends. Acknowledging that this uncertainty can feel frightening will assure patients that this is a normal reaction. Remind patients that they have learned skills that can be applied without continued assistance from the therapist, and that essentially, in learning these skills, patients have become their own therapist. It can also be encouraging to explicitly point out the work that patients may have done on their own, such as practicing emotion exposures.

References

Allen, L. B., White, K. S., Barlow, D. H., Shear, K. M., Gorman, J. M., & Woods, S. W. (2010). Cognitive-behavioral therapy (CBT) for panic disorder: Relationship of anxiety and depression comorbidity with treatment outcome. *Journal of Psychopathology and Behavioral Assessment, 32*(2), 185–192.

Barlow, D. H. (1988). *Anxiety and its disorders: The nature and treatment of anxiety and panic.* New York: Guilford Press.

Barlow, D. H. (1991). Disorders of emotion. *Psychological Inquiry, 2,* 58–71.

Barlow, D. H. (2000). Unraveling the mysteries of anxiety and its disorders from the perspective of emotion theory. *American Psychologist, 55,* 1247–1263.

Barlow, D. H. (2002). *Anxiety and its disorders: The nature and treatment of anxiety and panic* (2nd ed.). New York: Guilford Press.

Barlow, D. H. (2008). *Clinical handbook of psychological disorders: A step-by-step treatment manual* (4th ed.). London: Oxford University Press.

Barlow, D. H., Allen, L. B., & Basden, S. L. (2007). Psychological treatments for panic disorders, phobias, and generalized anxiety disorder. In P.E. Nathan & J.M. Gorman (Eds.), *A guide to treatments that work* (3rd ed., pp. 351–398). New York: Oxford University Press.

Barlow, D. H. & Cerny, J. A. (1988). *Psychological treatment of panic.* New York: Guilford Press.

Barlow, D. H., & Craske, M. G. (2000). *Mastery of your anxiety and panic (MAP-3): Client-workbook for anxiety and panic* (3rd ed.). San Antonio, TX: Graywind/Psychological Corporation.

Barlow, D. H., & Craske, M. G. (2006). *Mastery of your anxiety and panic: Client workbook (4th ed.).* New York: Oxford University Press.

Barlow, D. H., O'Brien, G. T., & Last, C. G. (1984). Couples treatment of agoraphobia. *Behavior Therapy, 15,* 41–58.

Beck, A. T. (1972). *Depression: Causes and treatment.* Philadelphia: University of Pennsylvania Press.

Beck, A. T., Epstein, N., Brown, G., & Steer, R. A. (1988). An inventory for measuring clinical anxiety: Psychometric properties. *Journal of Consulting and Clinical Psychology, 56,* 893–897.

Beck, A. T., Rush, A. J., Shaw, B. F., & Emery, G. (1979). *Cognitive therapy of depression.* New York: Guilford Press.

Beck, A. T., & Steer, R. A. (1990). Beck self-concept test. *Psychological Assessment, 2*(2), 191–197.

Beck, A. T., Steer, R. A., & Brown G. K. (1996). *Manual for the Beck Depression Inventory-II.* San Antonio, TX: Psychological Corporation.

Borkovec, T. D., Abel, J. L., & Newman, H. (1995). Effects of psychotherapy on comorbid conditions in generalized anxiety disorder. *Journal of Consulting and Clinical Psychology, 63,* 479–483.

Brown, T. A. (2007). Temporal course and structural relationships among dimensions of temperament and DSM-IV anxiety and mood disorder constructs. *Journal of Abnormal Psychology, 116,* 313–328.

Brown, T. A., Antony, M. M., & Barlow, D. H. (1995). Diagnostic comorbidity in panic disorder: Effect on treatment outcome and course of comorbid diagnoses following treatment. *Journal of Consulting and Clinical Psychology, 63,* 408–418.

Brown, T. A., & Barlow, D. H. (2009). A proposal for a dimensional classification system based on the shared features of the DSM-IV anxiety and mood disorders: Implications for assessment and treatment. *Psychological Assessment, 21*(3), 256–271.

Brown, T. A., Campbell, L. A., Lehman, C. L., Grisham, J. R., & Mancill, R. B. (2001). Current and lifetime comorbidity of the DSM-IV anxiety and mood disorders in a large clinical sample. *Journal of Abnormal Psychology, 110,* 49–58.

Brown, T. A., Chorpita, B. F., & Barlow, D. H. (1998). Structural relationships among dimensions of the DSM-IV anxiety and mood disorders and dimensions of negative affect, positive affect, and autonomic arousal. *Journal of Abnormal Psychology, 107,* 179–192.

Campbell-Sills, L. & Barlow, D. H. (2007). Incorporating emotion regulation into conceptualizations and treatments of anxiety and mood disorders. In J. J. Gross (Ed., pp. 542–560) *Handbook of emotion regulation.* NY, NY: Guilford Press.

Cerny, J. A., Barlow, D. H., Craske, M. G., & Himadi, W. G. (1987). Couples treatment of agoraphobia: A two-year follow-up. *Behavior Therapy, 18,* 401–415.

Chambless, D. L., & Steketee, G. (1999). Expressed emotion and behavior therapy outcome: A prospective study with obsessive-compulsive and agoraphobic outpatients. *Journal of Consulting and Clinical Psychology,* *67,* 658–665.

Chorpita, B. F., & Barlow, D. H. (1998). The development of anxiety: The role of control in the early environment. *Psychological Bulletin, 124,* 3–21.

Craske, M. G., Barlow, D. H., & O'Leary, T. (1992). *Mastery of your anxiety and worry.* San Antonio, TX: Graywind/Psychological Corporation.

Craske, M. G., Brown, T. A., Meadows, E. A., & Barlow, D. H. (1995). Uncued and cued emotions and associated distress in a college sample. *Journal of Anxiety Disorders, 9,* 125–137.

Craske, M. G., & Mystkowski, J. L. (2006). Exposure therapy and extinction: clinical studies. In M. G. Craske, D. Hermans, & D. Vansteenwegen (Eds.), *Fear and learning: Basic science to clinical application* (pp. 217–233). Washington, DC: APA Books.

Ellard, K. K., Fairholme, C. P., Boisseau, C. L., Farchione, T., & Barlow, D. H. (2010). Unified protocol for the transdiagnostic treatment of emotional disorders: Protocol development and initial outcome data. *Cognitive and Behavioral Practice, 17*(1), 88–101.

Etkin, A. & Wager, T. D. (2007). Functional neuroimaging of anxiety: A meta-analysis of emotional processing in PTSD, social anxiety disorder, and specific phobia. *The American Journal of Psychiatry, 164,* 1476–1488.

Fairholme, C. P., Boisseau, C. L., Ellard, K. K., Ehrenreich, J. T., & Barlow, D. H. (2009). Emotions, emotion regulation and psychological treatment: A Unified perspective. In A. Kring & D. Sloan (Eds.), *Emotion regulation and psychopathology.* New York: Guilford Press.

Frisch, M. B., Cornell, J., Villanueva, M. (1992). Clinical validation of the Quality of Life Inventory: A measure of life satisfaction for use in treatment planning and outcome assessment. *Psychological Assessment, 4*(1), 92–101.

Goodman, W. K., Price, L. H., Rasmussen, S. A., Mazure, C., Fleischmann, R. L., Hill, C., & Charney, D. S. (1989). The Yale-Brown Obsessive Compulsive Scale: I. Development, use, and reliability. *Archives of General Psychiatry, 46*(11), 1006–1011.

Gershuny, B. S., & Sher, K. J. (1998). The relation between personality and anxiety: Findings from a 3-year prospective study. *Journal of Abnormal Psychology, 107,* 252–262.

Gross J. J. (Ed.). (2007). *Handbook of emotion regulation.* New York: Guilford Press.

Gross, J. J., & Levenson, R. W. (1997). The acute effects of inhibiting negative and positive emotion. *Journal of Abnormal Psychology, 106,* 95–103.

Gross, J. J., & Thompson, R. A. (2007). Emotion regulation: Conceptual foundations. In J. J. Gross (Ed.), *Handbook of emotion regulation* (pp. 3–24). New York, NY: Guilford Press.

Hafner, R. J., & Marks, I. M. (1976). Exposure in vivo of agoraphobics: Contributions of diazepam, group exposure and anxiety evocation. *Psychological Medicine, 6,* 71–88.

Hays, R. D., Sherbourne, C. D., & Mazel, R. M. (1993). The Rand 36-item health survey 1.0. *Health Economics, 2,* 217–227.

Kasch, K. L., Rottenberg, J., Arnow, B. A., & Gotlib, I. H. (2002). Behavioral activation and inhibition systems and the severity and course of depression. *Journal of Abnormal Psychology, 111,* 589–597.

Kessler, R. C., Berglund, P., Demler, O. (2003). The epidemiology of major depressive disorder: Results from the National Comorbidity Survey Replication (NCS-R). *Journal of the American Medical Association, 289*(23), 3095–3105.

Kessler, R. C., Chiu, W. T., Demler, O., & Walters, E. (2005). Prevalence, severity, and comorbidity of 12-month DSM-IV disorders in the National Comorbidity Survey Replication. *Archives of General Psychiatry, 62,* 617–627.

Kessler, R. C., Nelson, C. B., McGonagle, K. A., Lui, J., Swartz, M., & Blazer, D. G. (1996). Comorbidity of DSM–III-R major depressive disorder in the general population: Results from the National Comorbidity Survey. *British Journal of Psychiatry, 168,* 17–30.

Kessler, R. C., Stang, P. E., Wittchen, H. U., Ustan, T. B., Roy-Byrne, P. P. & Walters, E. E. (1998). Lifetime panic-depression comorbidity in the National Comorbidity Survey. *Archives of General Psychiatry, 55,* 801–808.

Kring, A. M., & Sloan, D. M. (Eds.). (2010). *Emotion regulation and psychopathology: A transdiagnostic approach to etiology and treatment.* New York: Guilford Press.

Krueger, R. F., Watson, D., & Barlow, D. H. (2005). Introduction to the special section: Toward a dimensionally-based taxonomy of psychopathology. *Journal of Abnormal Psychology, 114,* 491–493.

Mattick, R. P., & Clarke, J. C. (1998). Development and validation of measures of social phobia scrutiny fear and social interaction anxiety. *Behaviour Research and Therapy, 36,* 455–470.

Meyer, T. J., Miller, M. L., Metzger, R. L., & Borkovec, T. D. (1990). Development and validation of the Penn State Worry Questionnaire. *Behaviour Research and Therapy, 28,* 487–495.

Miller, W. R., & Rollnick, S. (2002). *Motivational interviewing: Preparing people for change* (2nd ed.). New York: Guilford Press.

Monfils M. H, Cowansage, K. K, Klann, E., & LeDoux, J. E. (2009). Extinction-reconsolidation boundaries: key to persistent attenuation of fear memories. *Science, 324*(5929), 951–955.

Norman, S. B., Cissell, S. H., Means-Christensen, A. J., & Stein, M. B. (2006). Development and validation of an overall severity and impairment scale (OASIS). *Depression and Anxiety, 23,* 245–249.

Norton, P. J., & Price, E. C. (2007). A meta-analytic review of adult cognitive-behavioral treatment outcome across anxiety disorders. *The Journal of Nervous and Mental Disease, 195,* 521–531.

Otto, M. W., & Pollack, M. H. (2009). *Stopping anxiety medication: Therapist Guide.* New York: Oxford University Press.

Richards, J. M., & Gross, J. J. (2000). Emotion regulation and memory: The cognitive costs of keeping one's cool. *Journal of Personality and Social Psychology, 79,* 410–424.

Roemer, L., & Orsillo, S. M. (2007). An open trial of an acceptance-based behavior therapy for generalized anxiety disorder. *Behaviour Therapy, 38,* 72–85.

Rottenberg, J., & Gross, J. J. (2003). When emotion goes wrong: Realizing the promise of affective science. *Clinical Psychology: Science and Practice, 10,* 227–232.

Shear, M. K., Brown, T. A., Barlow, D. H., Money, R., Sholomskas, D. E., Woods, S. W., et al. (1997). Multicenter Collaborative Panic Disorder Severity Scale. *American Journal of Psychiatry, 154,* 1571–1575.

Shin, L.M., & Liberzon, I. (2010). The neurocircuitry of fear, stress, and anxiety disorders. *Neuropsychopharmacology Reviews, 35,* 169–191.

Steer, R. A., Ranieri, W. F., Beck, A. T., & Clark, D. A. (1993). Further evidence for the validity of the Beck Anxiety Inventory with psychiatric disorders. *Journal of Anxiety Disorders, 7,* 195–205.

Suárez, L., Bennett, S., Goldstein, C., & Barlow, D. H. (2009). Understanding anxiety disorders from a "triple vulnerabilities" framework. In M. M. Antony & M. B. Stein (Eds.), *Oxford handbook of anxiety and related disorders* (pp. 153–172). New York: Oxford.

Tsao, J. C. I., Lewin, M. R., & Craske, M. G. (1998). The effects of cognitive-behavior therapy for panic disorders on comorbid conditions. *Journal of Anxiety Disorders, 12*(4), 357–371.

Tsao, J. C. I., Mystkowski, J. L., & Zucker, B. G. (2002). Effects of cognitive-behavioral therapy for panic disorder on comorbid conditions: Replication and extension. *Behavior Therapy, 33*(4), 493–509.

Watson, D., Clark, L. A., & Carey, G. (1988). Positive and Negative Affectivity and their relation to anxiety and depressive disorders. *Journal of Abnormal Psychology, 97,* 346–353.

Wegner, D. M., Schneider, D. J., Carter, S. R., & White, T. L. (1987). Paradoxical effects of thought suppression. *Journal of Personality and Social Psychology, 53,* 5–13.

Westra, H. A., Arkowitz, H., & Dozois, D. J. A. (2009). Adding a motivational interviewing pretreatment to cognitive behavioral therapy for generalized anxiety disorder: A preliminary randomized controlled trial. *Journal of Anxiety Disorders, 23,* 1011–1184.

Westra, H. A., & Dozois, D. J. A. (2003). *Motivational interviewing adapted for anxiety/depression.* Unpublished treatment manual.

Westra, H. A., & Dozois, D. J. A. (2006). Preparing clients for cognitive behavioural therapy: A randomized pilot study of motivational interviewing for anxiety. *Cognitive Therapy and Research, 30,* 481–498.

Wilamowska, Z.A., Thompson-Hollands, J., Fairholme, C.P., Ellard, K.K., Farchione, T.J., & Barlow, D.H. (in press). Conceptual background, development, and preliminary data from the Unified Protocol for the Transdiagnostic Treatment of Emotional Disorders. *Depression and Anxiety.*

Zinbarg, R., Craske, M., & Barlow, D.H. (2006). *Therapist's guide for the mastery of your anxiety and worry program,* New York, NY: Oxford University Press.

Zinbarg, R., Lee, L.E., & Yoon, L. (2007). Dyadic predictors of outcome in a cognitive-behavioral program for patient generalized anxiety disorder in committed relationships: A "spoonful of sugar" and a dose of non-hostile criticism may help. *Behaviour Research and Therapy, 45*(4), 699–713.

About the Authors

David H. Barlow, PhD, is Professor of Psychology and Psychiatry, Founder, and Director Emeritus of the Center for Anxiety and Related Disorders at Boston University. He is editor-in-chief for the Treatments *ThatWork*™ series of therapist manuals and patient workbooks, as well as editor of *The Oxford Handbook of Clinical Psychology*.

Todd J. Farchione, PhD, is Research Assistant Professor in the Department of Psychology, Center for Anxiety and Related Disorders, Boston University.

Christopher P. Fairholme is an advanced doctoral student in the clinical psychology program at Boston University.

Kristen K. Ellard is an advanced doctoral student in the clinical psychology program at Boston University.

Christina L. Boisseau, PhD, is a Post Doctoral Fellow at the Alpert Medical School of Brown University, and completed her doctoral training in the clinical psychology program at Boston University.

Laura B. Allen, PhD, is Post Doctoral Research Scholar in the Pediatric Pain Program at UCLA's Collaborative Centers for Integrative Medicine, and completed her doctoral training in the clinical psychology program at Boston University.

Jill T. Ehrenreich-May, PhD, is Assistant Professor in the Department of Psychology at the University of Miami, and was previously Research Assistant Professor in the Department of Psychology, Center for Anxiety and Related Disorders, Boston University.